NEWMAN 101

NEWMAN101

An Introduction to
the Life and Philosophy
of John Cardinal Newman

Roderick Strange

Christian Classics   *Notre Dame, Indiana*

First published in the UK in 2008 as *Newman: A Mind Alive* by
Darton, Longman and Todd Ltd.
1 Spencer Court
140–142 Wandsworth High Street
London SW18 4JJ

Founded in 1865, Ave Maria Press is a ministry of the Indiana Province of Holy Cross.

www.christian-classics.com

ISBN-10 0-87061-247-6   ISBN-13 978-0-87061-247-3

Cover and text design by Brian C. Conley.

Cover image © Corbis Images

Printed and bound in the United States of America.

Library of Congress Cataloging-in-Publication Data

Strange, Roderick.
  Newman 101 : an introduction to the life and philosophy of John Cardinal Newman / Roderick Strange.
      p. cm.
  Includes bibliographical references (p.   ) and index.
  ISBN-13: 978-0-87061-247-3 (pbk.)
  ISBN-10: 0-87061-247-6 (pbk.)
  1. Newman, John Henry, 1801-1890. I. Title.

BX4705.N5S83 2008
282.092--dc22
[B]

                                        2008019651

*For
Anne-Marie,
Gill,
&
Alison*

Contents

Preface

When people are beatified or canonized, they are being offered to us as examples of holiness that we can follow with confidence. We need not suppose, however, that they have always been perfect. John Henry Newman once said as much about one of his theological heroes, St. Cyril of Alexandria, who, as a churchman, could be a ruthless political operator. We are not obliged, Newman remarked, to defend aspects of his ecclesiastical career: "It does not answer to call whity-brown, white" (*H.S.* ii, 342). Much more recently, Pope Benedict XVI echoed this same view. In his Wednesday audience on January 31, 2007, he observed, "The saints have not 'fallen from Heaven.' They are people like us, who also have complicated problems. Holiness does not consist in never having erred or sinned."[1] These are comforting words.

Newman himself has been a significant influence in my life. He may soon be beatified. In any case, my debt to him is far reaching. In this book, however, I am not suggesting that he was always right about everything. I do not feel obliged to champion and defend every position he took. "Holiness does not consist in never having erred or sinned." All the same, as his cause for beatification makes plain, he has a great deal to offer us.

I myself started to read Newman's work when I was eighteen, and I am reading and studying him still. What is more, after my ordination as a Catholic priest, I was given the chance to study his life and thought at some depth while engaged in doctoral research at Oxford University. Once that was completed, there were further opportunities: invitations began to arrive to write articles about aspects of his thought or give lectures on him or contribute chapters to books that were being prepared about him. In this way, over the years, a considerable amount of material has come together. I do not claim that it is startlingly original, but I would like to think that it offers helpful avenues into understanding Newman, his ideas, and his approach to problems and difficulties, which often enough we still struggle with today. Moreover, the benefits I have received from him are benefits I wish to share with others. In part, that wish prompted this book.

At the same time, this is not a collection, or even a selection, of my writings on Newman. It draws on them, but it edits, adapts, and rearranges them. Much of this material is new text, composed for the first time or developed from notes I have made for lectures and talks over the years. I am writing for people who are curious about Newman and would like to know more, and for those who enjoy reading but have little time for long books outside their own area of interest or expertise. I would like to think that those who have time to read only one book about Newman will find that this is the one. They may do so in part precisely because they can relate to something personal, Newman's influence on me, which I am happy to acknowledge.

It will be obvious, therefore, that this book does not pretend to be exhaustive, resolving disputes of scholarly detail between Newman specialists. Newman wrote so much that he created a rich arena for debate. Those controversies may have something to teach us, but they are not my concern here. I plan rather to offer access to his life and thought and experience by avoiding unnecessary detail. I shall draw attention instead to some of the elements that have impressed me and that may, therefore, still be valuable to others.

I will start with those points that made an impact on me, even from the beginning. Then I will sketch his life and consider more especially his search for the Church; that search itself was lifelong. Next, we need to be aware of the thinking that underpinned his thought. This chapter is titled "A Mind Alive." It is central, but not because Newman can be reduced to an icy intellectual. His mind was alive because it reached out to touch the heart and engage the whole person. That union of mind and heart and person will be evident time and again in what follows.

Then his interpretation of papal infallibility, the way he presented teaching about Mary both as an Anglican and as a Catholic, and the value he placed on the role of the laity in the Church are all issues that can be seen as controversial, but the way Newman treated them points as well to his care for ecumenism, his sensitivity to the need for the Church to be one. After probing these issues, we can return to the man himself, his awareness of divine providence, his preaching about faith, and his life as a witness to holiness. And at the end, as a kind of coda, there is a reflection on his poem "The Dream of Gerontius."

Although in preparing this particular text I have not needed to visit Father Paul Chavasse and the fathers at the Birmingham Oratory, I have clear memories of their generous hospitality when my Newman studies were in their infancy. And whenever I have visited since, they have always received me warmly. I would also like to pay tribute to Gerard Tracey, who has died, and to Brother Francis McGrath, F.M.S., for their work in completing the publication of Newman's *Letters and Diaries* and for the kind assistance they have always been ready to offer me.

I am conscious too of the debts I owe to others who have studied Newman and whose friendship and insight have encouraged me, people like Bishop Geoffrey Rowell, Nicholas Lash, Ian Ker, Sheridan Gilley, Joyce Sugg, and Stephen Prickett. There are too many to mention, but no list of mine must omit two who have died, John Coulson and the incomparable Stephen Dessain. And I wish also to thank my friend and colleague at the Beda College, Fr. John Breen. Chapter by chapter, as each was completed, was passed before his keen, critical, but non-specialist eye. His help was invaluable, and I am deeply grateful to him.

And finally, there is the dedication. Newman had three sisters, and so have I. The eldest, Anne-Marie, I never knew for she died at birth, but she is no less loved because of that. And the other two, Gill and Alison, have filled my life with friendship, love, and laughter. I thank them with love. I am proud to dedicate this book to my sisters.

Acknowledgments

Some parts of this book have been adapted from earlier articles of mine in the *Ampleforth Journal*, the *Clergy Review*, *Priests and People*, *Louvain Studies*, *Marian Studies*, *Newman-Studies*, *One in Christ*, and the *Canadian Catholic Review*, and from contributions to Perry Butler, ed., *Pusey Rediscovered* (London, 1983); Rosario La Delfa and Alessandro Magno, eds., *Luce nella Solitudine* (Palermo, 1989); *Rosario La Delfa*, ed., *Il Viaggio e La Malattia di Newman in Sicilia* (Palermo, 1991); and Paul Vaiss, ed., *Newman: From Oxford to the People* (Leominster, 1996). The final chapter is based on "The Flame of Love," which appeared in *Priests and People* in December 1990 and was originally broadcast on BBC Radio 3 on September 16, 1990. I am grateful for permission to make use of this material again here.

Unless stated otherwise, scriptural quotations have been taken from the New Revised Standard Version, Catholic Edition, published by Geoffrey Chapman in 1993, and quotations from Vatican Council documents have been taken from Norman Tanner, ed., *Decrees of the Ecumenical Councils*, 2 vols. (London and Washington, 1990).

Abbreviations

The abbreviations I have used are those that have become standard and are listed in C. S. Dessain et al (eds.), *The Letters and Diaries of John Henry Newman* i–xxxii, Oxford and London: Thomas Nelson, 1961–2007; hereafter *L.D.*

Page references are taken from the Uniform Edition of Newman's works. Where a second reference is given in square brackets, it is taken from a subsequent critical edition, noted below.

Apo.	*Apologia pro Vita Sua*
Ari.	*The Arians of the Fourth Century*
Ath. i, ii	*Select Treatises of St. Athanasius*
A.W.	*Autobiographical Writings*
D.A.	*Discussions and Arguments on Various Subjects*
Dev.	*An Essay on the Development of Christian Doctrine*
Diff. i, ii	*Certain Difficulties Felt by Anglicans in Catholic Teaching*
Ess. i, ii	*Essays Critical and Historical*
G.A.	*An Essay in Aid of a Grammar of Assent*
H.S. i, ii, iii	*Historical Sketches*
Idea	*The Idea of a University Defined and Illustrated*
Jfc.	*Lectures on the Doctrine of Justification*
M.D.	*Meditations and Devotions of the Late Cardinal Newman*
Mix.	*Discourses Addressed to Mixed Congregations*
O.S.	*Sermons Preached on Various Occasions*
Prepos.	*Present Position of Catholics in England*
P.S. i–viii	*Parochial and Plain Sermons*
S.D.	*Sermons Bearing on Subjects of the Day*
T.T.	*Tracts Theological and Ecclesiastical*

U.S.	*Fifteen Sermons Preached Before the University of Oxford*
V.M. i, ii	*The Via Media*
V.V.	*Verses on Various Occasions*

Critical Editions

Martin J. Svalgic, ed., *Apologia pro Vita Sua* (Oxford, 1967)

Ian T. Ker, ed., *An Essay in Aid of a Grammar of Assent* (Oxford, 1985)

Ian T. Ker, ed., *The Idea of a University* (Oxford, 1976)

H. D. Weidner, ed., *The "Via Media" of the Anglican Church* (Oxford, 1990)

1

Have You Read Any Newman?

(i)

It was my good fortune when I went up to Oxford in 1970 to study Newman to find that Father Stephen Dessain, that prince among Newman scholars, had agreed to be my supervisor. Stephen was a member of the Birmingham Oratory, which Newman had founded. He was deeply devoted to Newman, and his knowledge of Newman's writings was without equal. His small biography, *John Henry Newman*, which was first published in 1966, remains the best brief biography of the cardinal, and the twenty-one volumes of Newman's *Letters and Diaries*, which he edited and saw published between 1961 and his death in 1976, bear witness to his grasp of the corpus. Although he assisted countless other people with their research, I was to be his only full-time student.

Stephen and I knew each other a little already from his visits to Rome while I was a student at the English College at the Vatican; he attended my priestly ordination on December 21, 1969. By chance that day was the anniversary of his own initiation into the religious life. Ever generous, he brought me as a present the collection of Newman's Oratorian papers, which had been edited by Dom Placid Murray and published the year before with the title *Newman the Oratorian*.[1] Inside he had written Newman's words about God's hidden saints and their influence: "Say they are few, such high Christians; and what follows? They are enough to carry on God's noiseless work" (*U.S.*, 96). While Newman was referring to the saints, I have no doubt that Stephen was thinking of Newman. And this book is in part my attempt to explore Newman's influence on me, his part for me in "God's noiseless work."

I can precisely date the time and place where it all began. It was the morning of March 30, 1964, and I was on a Roman bus on my way to the Alban Hills, south of the city. It was Easter Monday. I had come to the English College as a seminarian the previous October, and that Monday I was going to Palazzola, the college's villa, for a week's break after Easter before lectures began again. I was traveling with Tony Cornish, a fellow student and, since 1967, a priest of the Plymouth Diocese in Southwest England. At one point in our conversation, Tony turned to me and asked, "Have you read any Newman, Rod?" I had not. I had only the vaguest idea of who Newman was. I had seen portraits. He then told me about author Meriol Trevor's 1962 critically acclaimed two-volume biography, which had been published and which the college library had just acquired.[2] When I got back to Rome, I went to find it and decided to read it that summer during our long vacation. And I did.

What I read captivated me. I went on at once to read Newman himself. I began with his autobiography, *Apologia pro Vita Sua*, in which he gave his account of his journey to Catholicism, and I wrote my own extended summary of it as a way of trying to grasp a little more clearly the sequence of events. It would be fair to say that I have been reading and studying Newman's work ever since. There has been much else, of course, but Newman has never been too far away.

What was it that impressed me? In many ways, as I have said, this entire book is an answer to that question, but let me begin by mentioning three aspects in particular that struck me almost immediately.

(ii)

First, like most people, I love a good story, and I found the story of Newman's life enthralling. It revolves around the twin ingredients of controversy and surprise. The young Newman, though shy, was recognized as brilliant. When he took his degree, however, he managed only to scrape together a pass. Intensity and overwork had drained him. Nevertheless, the following year he was elected a Fellow of Oriel, which at that time was regarded as the very cream of Oxford intellectual society.

As a college tutor, Newman believed that his care for his pupils should extend beyond simply the teaching he gave them. Something more personal, a moral dimension, was needed. Many years later he stated his view plainly: "An academical system without the personal influence of teachers upon pupils, is an arctic winter; it will create an ice-bound, petrified, cast-iron University, and nothing else" (*H.S.* iii, 74). A view that is commonplace today was seen then as a reform so radical that he had his pupils withdrawn. And one ironic consequence of that action was for him to find himself with time available, when the moment came some years later, to devote himself wholeheartedly to the Oxford Movement, which aimed to renew the Anglican Church of England by restoring to it its share in the Catholic tradition.

When the Movement began, he was its driving force. But then he found himself drawn by his own arguments, along with a series of events, to doubt the very position for which he was so eloquent an advocate. Some years later, after anguished study and reflection, he ceased being an Anglican and was received into the Roman Catholic Church. That was in 1845. This decision was as painful as it was dramatic, for it caused a parting from friends that only long years and abiding affection on both sides would overcome.

Catholicism, however, was no safe haven for him. Further controversies ensued.

After ordination in Rome, he established the Congregation of the Oratory in Birmingham and London, but later his plans there were marred by an unhappy dispute between the two houses. Then during a series of lectures in 1851, he took the opportunity to respond to the scandalous allegations against Catholics that were being made in England by a former Dominican friar, Giacinto Achilli, and he was tried for libel. The evidence that could have cleared Newman had been mislaid by Cardinal Nicholas Wiseman, the Archbishop of Westminster, and a prejudiced jury found Newman guilty. Many people were outraged, and the verdict prompted the British newspaper the *Times* to observe that Roman Catholics could no longer have faith in British justice.

During this time Newman was also working to found a university in Dublin, Ireland, at the invitation of the Irish bishops but was consistently being denied the support he needed to make the venture succeed. Then in 1859, the year following his return to England from Ireland, he was persuaded to accept the editorship of the Catholic periodical the *Rambler*, which the bishops regarded at the time as being too critical; he was judged to be a safer pair of hands and acceptable to both the bishops and the periodical's proprietors. His attempt to calm anxieties, however, misfired, and almost at once he was asked to resign. The situation deteriorated further for him because soon afterward an article of his own on consulting the laity brought him under suspicion in Rome. His readiness to answer objections was not passed on to the Church authorities, and he remained under a cloud of suspicion there for some years.

At the end of 1863, matters came to a head. Anglican priest and critic of the Catholic clergy Charles Kingsley accused Newman of indifference to truth, and there poured out from Newman his *Apologia pro Vita Sua*. That controversy marked a turning point, at least with regard to the respect his contemporaries held for him. Yet there were more controversies to follow. His plans for establishing an oratory in Oxford were encouraged at first but then frustrated, and notably his moderate interpretation of the doctrine of papal infallibility brought him into conflict with

Archbishop (later Cardinal) Manning's, another Catholic convert from Anglicanism, extreme ultramontane[3] view. But finally in old age, Newman's life became more serene.

In 1878, Trinity College, Oxford, where he had been an undergraduate student, invited him to become its first honorary fellow, and so he visited Oxford again for the first time in thirty-two years. And then the following year, the new pope, Leo XIII, named him a cardinal. Old wounds were healing; the cloud of suspicion was lifted from him forever.

As a young man, beginning my preparation for ministerial priesthood, it seemed to me a stirring tale, an example of love for the truth and fidelity to Christ and the Church, and it compelled my admiration.

A second aspect that caught my attention was the fact that Newman was English. It may help to remember that when I began reading him, the Second Vatican Council was in progress. The Council was encouraging a growing awareness of the local church, and Newman's personality and approach to many issues gave a clear example of what that could mean for England. The point is not chauvinistic. His influence in other countries is too well known for that. It is simply a matter of acknowledging that when the Church in Council was trying to recognize what each culture could contribute to its life, Newman supplied a particular illustration of what the English contribution might be. On one occasion, years later, some friends who were not Catholics were joking with me by saying that Newman had never really been a Catholic but was always an Anglican at heart. I responded by saying that on the contrary, I felt Newman had shown how being English and Catholic were compatible. It was just banter, but I may have struck a nerve because there was a sudden silence and the subject was changed.

Thinking of banter, it is perhaps worth adding here that most people don't usually associate Newman with humor. But I found that preconception mistaken. Let me offer some examples.

On holiday in the Mediterranean in 1832, there was a splendidly comic account of his seasickness: "the worst of seasickness," he observed in a long letter to his mother on December 23, "is the sympathy which all things on board have with the illness, as if they were seasick too." He goes on to describe the movement of table and chairs—swing, swing—and the motion of the glasses, knives, and forks on the tables, with wine spilling—swing, swing—and trying to hide the misery he felt, until he could do so no longer, but when he got up, he couldn't move because the ship was moving, and when he finally made his berth, the door wouldn't shut, then "bang, bang, you slam your fingers." Then, when he lay down, there was the noise of the bulkheads, the noises of the gale, "creaking, clattering, shivering, and dashing," not to mention the bilge water, which he called an "unspeakable nuisance," set in motion by the storm and draining down to the bottom of the boat (*L.D.* iii, 159). The whole passage is masterly. And his letters generally are full of comic observation, such as his comment on William Wilberforce's false teeth and his habit of throwing "the whole set out of the gums upon his tongue, and [chewing] them, as an infant might a coral" (*L.D.* xx, 261). And there is the story of Newman laughing just before sending off the final proofs of *An Essay in Aid of a Grammar of Assent*, which he had dedicated to his friend Edward Bellasis "in remembrance of a long, equable, sunny friendship." Just in time he noticed that the dedication recalled instead "a long squabble and funny friendship." There is plenty more.[4]

And a third element that impressed me early on was Newman's instinct for pastoral care. I soon discovered that when people knew anything about him at all, they tended to think in stereotypes, contrasting him with his contemporary Henry Manning. Manning was seen as the practical one, involved in the world's affairs, while Newman was regarded as intellectual and remote.[5] But the reality was very different. I was struck by Newman's practicality, his commitment to pastoral matters, and the administrative skill that went with it.

When he took up his first curacy at St. Clement's in Oxford, he was an earnest evangelical Anglican who, while not believing in predestination, was convinced that more people were damned

Heart speaks to heart

than were saved. But by caring for his parishioners, he learned otherwise. "How could the majority of such good people be destined for hell?" he wondered; that could not be true. Then, as I noted earlier, when he became a tutor at Oriel, he could not see that role as a matter merely of intellectual instruction. And later as vicar of the University Church and leader of the Oxford Movement, he was full of pastoral energy. His preaching from that time has become legendary. "It is of the essence of the Movement," theologian and scholar Owen Chadwick has observed, "that its best writing should be enshrined in parochial sermons."[6]

After his reception into full communion with the Catholic Church in 1845, this same pastoral energy drove him on. He established the oratories in Birmingham and London and founded the Catholic University in Dublin. He also set up the Oratory School for boys. In all these projects, his administrative gifts, as well as his pastoral instinct, were fully engaged. That pastoral instinct was also evident decisively in his vast correspondence with an astonishing range of people and found further expression in his other writings, where his devotion to what was real, as he would say, rather than the merely notional, was always evident. He had no time for theories, however splendid, if they could make no impact. "I say plainly I do not want to be converted by a smart syllogism," he wrote in *A Grammar of Assent*, which he published in 1870, "if I am asked to convert others by it I say plainly I do not care to overcome their reason without touching their hearts" (*G.A.*, 425 [273]).

Such pastoral commitment could hardly fail to inspire me as a young man as my own preparation for ministerial priesthood gathered momentum. And then there was something else, something interior.

(iii)

Effective pastoral work needs to be more than activity. It must be in tune with the person within; it must flow from spirituality. Reading Newman, I soon became aware of his extraordinarily

vivid sense of God's existence and presence. His pastoral instinct
and energy were undeniable; in no way was he in flight from practical demands; nevertheless, it could be said that there was a sense
for him in which the unseen world had a greater reality than the
seen. Early in his *Apologia*, he described himself as coming to rest
when young "in the thought of two and two only absolute and
luminously self-evident beings, myself and my Creator" (*Apo.*, 4
[18]). In other words, he was as sure of God's existence as he was
of his own. Few of us would probably be able to make such a
claim, or at least we would not make it in those terms. All the
same, it is wonderful to be encouraged, as I was by Newman at
that time, as I prepared myself for priestly ministry, to look beyond the visible world and nurture a sense of the world unseen.
Sensitivity to the unseen stimulates that longing for God, which is
indispensable for a life of prayer.

Styles and approaches in prayer are very varied. Some people
love the company of others when they pray, as well as the stimuli
of words and music. My usual preference would be for stillness.
One image of Newman's has never failed to help me. In a sermon
called "Equanimity," he asks: "Did you ever look at an expanse of
water, and observe the ripples on the surface? Do you think that
disturbance penetrates below it?" He goes on to speak of tempests
and scenes of horror and distress at sea, but remarks, "The founda-
tions of the ocean, the vast realms of water which girdle the earth,
are as tranquil and as silent in the storm as in a calm." He uses it
as an image for the souls of those who are holy: "They have a well
of peace springing up within them unfathomable" (*P.S.* v, 69).
As the passage continues, he acknowledges how troubled we may
sometimes be in fact, and indeed such catastrophes like the tsu-
nami in the Indian Ocean in 2004 and Hurricane Katrina in 2005
may seem to qualify the image further; but these tragic events cannot simply cancel that peace altogether. This appeal to tranquility
in the deepest sense has given me encouragement to persevere in
prayer beyond any immediate difficulties in order to discover the
strength and stillness of God.

Hand in hand with this belief in God's existence and presence, as well as the call to prayerfulness, went Newman's sense of God's providence: the Lord is not only close to us, he cares for us. No one can read Newman's life carefully and believe he thought otherwise. The idea may seem bewildering to many people today, implying divine intrusion into the natural course of events, or their manipulation. But that was not how Newman saw it. He believed that God had a plan for each of us, a plan made real by his presence among us—a plan and a presence that we see as providential when we recognize it within our lives. We call providential those moments or occasions in our lives when we become aware of God's will for us. They are privileged demonstrations of his abiding presence.

It took a long while for my own appreciation of providence to reach this stage, but I remember clearly how it began. I was reading one of Newman's sermons and came to these words: "God beholds thee individually, whoever thou art. He 'calls thee by thy name.' He sees thee and understands thee, as He made thee." He goes on, concluding, "Thou dost not love thyself better than He loves thee" (*P.S.* iii, 124–125). If time has mellowed the initial impact of those words, it has not diminished their reality for me. We will explore Newman's understanding of providence more fully later.[7]

Fascination with Newman's long life and work in England, as well as his pastoral instinct, on the one hand, and his profound spirituality, on the other, have had their influence on me. Before continuing further, however, let me mention one other way, specific and practical, in which I have found myself following his example over the years.

(iv)

When Newman published the first volume of his *Parochial Sermons* in 1834, the custom was to include in some way the whole range of Christian doctrine, but he was criticized because he had placed emphasis on some aspects of the Anglican Church's teaching and ignored others. His friend Samuel Wilberforce took him to task. He wrote to complain that Newman was too severe in his demands for an evident change of heart and that he had not made sufficient allowance for the work of the Spirit in bringing sinners to repentance. But Newman remained unmoved. It is not necessary to go into the details of that controversy here. It is enough to recognize that Newman was not intending to deny the power of the Spirit working in people; however, he felt the need at that time to bring out the importance of an individual's response to grace. That was the aspect he wished to emphasize. There would be opportunities for other aspects at other times. And the particular point that impressed me was his assertion that he could not deal with everything at once. As he told Wilberforce: "I lay it down as a fundamental Canon, that a Sermon to be effective must be imperfect." He could not bring in every doctrine everywhere. At one time certain elements would be considered, at another time others. However, he claimed, "No one, who *habitually* hears me, ought to have any other than the whole Scripture impression" (*L.D.* v, 38). The plan was to proceed part by part; the result would be an account of the whole. Working in very different circumstances, which is precisely what I have tried to do.

Both as a priest in a parish and particularly as a university chaplain, I have sought to supply a whole account of the Church's teaching. It has not generally been practicable to do so by offering a series of extended lectures. Instead it has had to be done gradually, through homilies and talks, assembling little by little the pieces of the jigsaw. And there is evidence of the outcome. In 1986 I published a small book called *The Catholic Faith*. It was essentially a reworking into a whole of homilies and sermons, lectures and talks, that I had been giving at the Oxford University Chaplaincy. It considers Christ and the Church, the sacraments and the virtues, Mary and the Trinity. A later book, *Living Catholicism*, published in 2001, emerged in much the same way. They have generally been well received, and the material in them was gathered by following Newman's approach.[8]

(v)

Many other aspects of Newman's life, like the valuing of friends, and of his thought, like the role of theological reflection, and of his experience, like love and care for the unity of the Church, have made their mark on me over the years. They will become evident as this book unfolds. And there have, of course, been other influences besides Newman, some of them no doubt qualifying and adapting what I have learned from him, but it would be dishonest of me to disclaim the impact he has had on my life and priestly ministry.

Some years after I had been ordained and while I was studying him in Oxford as a graduate priest, a friend asked me why I did not quote him more often when I preached. The question took me by surprise, and I had to think carefully to find the answer. Then I realized that in fact I was quoting him frequently, but rarely word for word. His influence goes deeper. My debt is incalculable, my gratitude profound.

2

Newman's Path

(i)

Newman was born on February 21, 1801, and died on August 11, 1890. It was a long and involved life, profound and complex. In October 1963, when Pope Paul VI was beatifying the Passionist priest Dominic Barberi, who had received Newman into the Catholic Church, he paused in his address to speak of Newman directly. He described him as someone who

> in full consciousness of his mission—"I have a work to do"—and guided solely by love of the truth and fidelity to Christ, traced an itinerary, the most toilsome, but also the greatest, the most meaningful, the most conclusive, that human thought ever traveled during the [nineteenth] century, indeed one might say during the modern era, to arrive at the fullness of wisdom and of peace.[1]

These words were highly charged. Stephen Dessain remarked to me later that it sounded as though the pope were beatifying

Newman rather than Dominic. Be that as it may, he was clearly aware of Newman's journey.

It is not easy to follow the path of so full a life, but a sketch is needed to provide some context for the issues to be considered later. Various approaches are possible.

I have mentioned already my early fascination with the contrasts in Newman's life, the pattern of expectation and disappointment: the brilliant undergraduate who scarcely manages to get a degree; the tutor at Oriel who has his pupils withdrawn; the leader of the Oxford Movement who becomes a Roman Catholic; the distinguished convert who is not trusted fully and whose talents are misused; then finally, the unexpected years as a cardinal when the cloud is lifted and he is valued and treated with respect. Throughout all that time, Newman was in search of the Church. For him the guiding question was: where was the Body of Christ to be found most fully? He wished to be a member. And when he felt he had answered that question and then had acted upon it, becoming a Catholic in 1845, there were still long years to be lived of maturing, suffering, and humiliation.

There are, perhaps, three main stages to this intriguing life. Until 1833 he was in search of himself; the years from 1833 to 1845 were for him a kind of crucible; after that the consequences of his decision to become a Catholic were played out.

(ii)

When people speak of Newman's conversion, they are usually referring to the events of October 8 and 9, 1845, that windswept night when Father Dominic Barberi, drenched by rain from his journey exposed to the weather, arrived in Littlemore, the village where Newman had made his home after resigning his Oriel fellowship and retiring to lay communion as an Anglican. He began to hear Newman's confession that evening, and it continued the following morning. Then he received him into the Roman Catholic Church. That conversion, however, had been preceded by others.

Newman had been brought up as a normally devout Anglican who read his bible and knew it well. In 1816, however, when he was fifteen and at school, he became ill, the first of three significant illnesses of these early years. While recovering, he was given a number of Calvinist books and had an experience of conversion. He believed he was "elected to eternal glory." It was the time when he came to rest in "the thought of two and two only absolute and luminously self-evident beings, myself and my Creator" (*Apo.*, 4 [17–18]). Nothing dramatic seems to have occurred outwardly; there was nothing wildly enthusiastic that could be likened to baptism in the Spirit or speaking in tongues; but the immediate effects of that experience remained for a while and then faded over a period of about five years. It made Newman earnestly evangelical. This was the state of the young man who went up to Oxford as an undergraduate the following year.

He was expected to do brilliantly when he came to take his degree in 1820, but in the event it was a disaster. He had overworked, become overtired and tense. As he recorded much later, he "lost his head, utterly broke down, and after vain attempts for several days had to retire." He secured his degree, but barely. He had failed altogether in mathematics, which was his best subject, and only managed to scrape through in classics (*A.W.*, 47).

What was he to do next? His poor degree made the legal career he considered seem impossible, and so he decided to be ordained instead. In due course, he became an Anglican deacon in 1824 and a priest the following year. But in the meantime, in spite of his poor degree, he had made up his mind to stand for a fellowship at Oriel, then the most intellectually prestigious of the Oxford colleges. He was successful and was elected on April 12, 1822. It was not so much the quality of his papers that swayed the electors, but the character of his scholarship. More than twenty years later, Edward Copleston, who had been provost of Oriel at the time, recalled it, describing Newman as "not even a good classical scholar, yet in mind and powers of composition, and in taste and knowledge, . . . decidedly superior" to other competitors who had previously gained better degrees as undergraduates (*A.W.*, 64). And so

Newman found himself a fellow of Oriel and familiar with some of the most distinguished men in Oxford at that time.

One of them was Richard Whately, who was to become the Archbishop of Dublin in the Church of Ireland. He was colorful in dress, witty in speech, and trenchant in argument. He was also renowned, in Newman's words much later, as "singularly gracious to undergraduates and young masters" (*A.W.*, 66). He took Newman under his wing and was the ideal person for bringing the reserved young man out of his shell. Newman was a great listener and Whately a great talker. Moreover, Whately liked to talk logic, and he, perhaps more than anyone else, helped Newman develop his own formidable forensic skill. Samuel Taylor Coleridge, famous for his poem *The Rime of the Ancient Mariner*, once remarked, "Every man is born an Aristotelian, or a Platonist. I do not think it possible that any one born an Aristotelian can become a Platonist; and I am sure no born Platonist can change into an Aristotelian."[2] Historian David Newsome suggests, however, that if there is an exception to Coleridge's dictum, it is Newman, "born a Platonist," but through his education "become an Aristotelian."[3] And if Newsome is right, then Whately more than anyone else was responsible for helping him learn how the vision whole could be divided into parts.

Subsequent events made Newman and Whately drift apart, but they were close for about ten years. During the earlier years in particular, Newman relished the atmosphere of the Oriel Senior Common Room, where they met and which was said to "stink of logic." It is easy to imagine him, roused from his shyness, becoming aware of his intellectual gifts and taking delight in using them. What could be more natural? This was the time when he fell under the spell of intellectual excellence. That reigned supreme. But its influence did not last. Three factors combined to change his attitude.

First, he became unwell again. Overwork, family worries, college business, and examining responsibilities caused him to collapse in November 1827. Then, a few weeks later, on January 5, 1828, his youngest sister, Mary, whom he loved tenderly, died suddenly. Her death shattered him. It is easy to understand why: to read her letters, light but perceptive, humorous and loving, is to realize how lovable she must have been (*L.D.* ii, 38–39). His own ill health, therefore, and Mary's death forced him to take stock of what really mattered. How could intellectual excellence compare with the loss of a beloved sister, or even to damage to his good health? And at that very time, other Oriel friendships were developing, drawing him away from Whately. In particular he was coming to know the studious Edward Pusey, the saintly John Keble, and more immediately the irrepressible Hurrell Froude, who was to die prematurely from consumption in 1836. Their influence would grow, and he would come increasingly to share with them a devotion to the Catholic tradition within the Church of England that was to be fundamental to the Oxford Movement. Here was another conversion. He was no longer dazzled by the intellect in isolation. Insofar as he could be said to have flirted with rationalism, the flirtation was over.

The college business, which had preoccupied Newman when he took ill in 1827, was the need to elect a new provost, a new head of House for Oriel. When the time came, Newman voted for Edward Hawkins, who was in fact elected. He had been kind to Newman when he first became a fellow. And Hawkins was in a way pivotal at this stage of Newman's life.

In the first place, it was through Hawkins that Newman had come to an understanding of baptism as new birth, independent of personal experience, and so had been helped to shed his earlier severe evangelicalism, and while listening to Hawkins when he was an undergraduate, Newman began to learn from him the significance of tradition. Then second, Hawkins had been the Vicar of St. Mary the Virgin, the University Church, but when he became provost, he had had to resign. Newman succeeded him and gained thereby a place of influence. It was from the pulpit of St. Mary's that he was to deliver some of his most memorable sermons. And finally, it was Hawkins who was opposed to Newman's view of a tutor's duties and, as provost, opposed that view successfully, forcing Newman to have his students withdrawn. And so it was that when the Oxford Movement began, Newman found he had the time and freedom at his disposal to commit himself to its cause without reserve. In his *Apologia*, while Newman acknowledged their differences, he also declared his abiding affection for Hawkins personally. And Hawkins wrote a kind letter, thanking him (*Apo.*, 8–10 [21–22; 485–486]).

In 1832, however, deprived of pupils and, therefore, without teaching responsibilities, Newman was able to take a vacation. He went with Hurrell Froude, who by that time was already starting to sicken with the consumption that would eventually kill him, and with Archdeacon Froude, Hurrell's father, on a Mediterranean holiday. They toured widely, including, for Newman, a first visit to Rome, where they called in at the English College and met Nicholas Wiseman, who was then the rector and who would later become a cardinal and the first Archbishop of Westminster. Newman was fascinated by the whole experience, but questioning. He wrote many poems during the trip. One begins:

> O that thy creed were sound!
> For thou dost soothe the heart, thou Church of Rome,
> By thy unwearied watch and varied round
> Of service, in thy Saviour's holy home. (*V.V.*, 153)

Most of all, however, he loved Sicily. He had visited it with the Froudes before going on to Rome and been enchanted by it. So, when they were set to continue their journey toward England, he changed his plans, left them, and returned to visit the island once more. There he fell ill again, the third major illness of these early years. He felt guilty. He saw it as a punishment for his willfulness, selfishly deserting his friends to follow his own desire. Indeed, he might have died. But in his sickness he was also overcome by a sense of mission: "I have a work to do," words recalled by Pope Paul when he was beatifying Dominic Barberi. He recovered and set off for England. Becalmed in the Strait of Bonifacio on June 16, 1833, he composed his poem "The Pillar of the Cloud," which is better known now as the hymn "Lead, Kindly Light." In it he acknowledges the darkness and his own pride but trusts in the power that has blessed him and will lead him on, "o'er moor and fen, o'er crag and torrent, till the night is gone" (*V.V.*, 156–157). He arrived back in England on July 8.

These early years, marked by maturing views, from evangelicalism through a kind of rationalism to a more harmonious sense of the Church of England as also Catholic, and scarred by personal crisis, sickness, and death, had brought Newman to a turning point. He had sensed it while he was ill in Sicily: there was work to do. Then, six days after his return, on July 14, 1833, John Keble preached the Assize Sermon at Oxford.

(iii)

For Newman that sermon signaled the start of the Oxford Movement, but in fact events were less clear cut. For some time there had been those in the Church of England who were afraid it would come to be controlled by the state. How, then, could it be free to proclaim the gospel, should conflict arise? And conflict, they felt, had then arisen. The issue, soon forgotten in itself, was Parliament's reordering of the Church in Ireland through the suppression of some dioceses. In practice, it was an entirely sensible matter; in principle, however, it was seen as undermining the independence of the Church, the state interfering with the successors of the apostles. Keble's sermon, titled "National Apostasy," became a trigger for action.

Some gathered at Hadleigh parsonage in Suffolk and discussed the forming of committees around the country that would help spread Catholic principles within the Anglican Church. Newman did not attend the meeting and was impatient with the outcome. "Living movements do not come of committees," he remarked in his *Apologia*, and with others he set about writing brief articles instead, summoning the Church of England to an understanding of itself based on Catholic principles (*Apo.*, 39 [46]). These were the tracts that gave the Oxford Movement its other name, the Tractarian Movement. In the beginning, he had them printed himself, only leaflet size at the start, and rode around the countryside from parsonage to parsonage distributing them.

Fundamental to the Oxford Movement was care for the integrity of the Church. That was the cause Newman was championing. He had no doubt that the Church of England was a branch of the great Church Catholic: Roman, Eastern, and Anglican; but he saw it under threat from evangelicals and liberals and from high and dry churchmen who had lost a sense of its rich heritage.

To remedy that loss, he gave his own account of the Anglican Church. He presented it as a *via media*, a middle way, between Roman excess, on the one hand, and Protestant error, on the other. He distilled his approach in a series of lectures he delivered at St. Mary's and then published in 1837. These were his *Lectures on the Prophetical Office of the Church*. The core of his position rested on three fundamental convictions.

First, he described the Church as indefectible but not infallible. Infallibility, he argued, was characteristic of the Church united, but since it had been scarred by division, that promise had been lost. Nevertheless, the Church is guided divinely to teach essential, saving truth indefectibly (*V.M.* i, 201, 190 [228, 219]). Second, to identify that truth, he appealed to antiquity, to the scriptures and the Church of the Fathers, to that teaching that had been taught always, everywhere, and by all, *quod semper, quod ubique, quod ab omnibus*, as the creed for admission and as the rule of teaching (*V.M.* i, 222 [245]). And third, he drew out the way this essential gospel teaching had been handed down in the Creed from bishop to bishop and so was called Episcopal tradition, while there was also another vast, less formal tradition, "pervading the Church like an atmosphere," that interprets revelation and unfolds its mysteries; this tradition he called prophetical (*V.M.* i, 249–251 [267–269]). That, in brief, was the basis of the understanding of the Church that Newman advocated. Even at the outset, he was aware of a weakness: while "Popery and Protestantism are real religions," he observed, ". . . the *Via Media*, viewed as an integral system, has never had existence except on paper" (*V.M.* i, 16 [70–71]). Nevertheless, for six years, in spite of grueling controversy, all was well. He championed his cause under a clear sky. Then a cloud appeared.

Newman valued precedents. Present integrity was secure because it was reflected in the past. During a long vacation in 1839, however, while he was reading at leisure, studying the history of Monophysitism, a fifth century heresy, he suddenly became alarmed. The Monophysite understanding of Christ, that in Christ there was only one nature, the divine, had been condemned. At the same time, the Monophysites themselves had remained utterly opposed to the Eutychians, whose account of the one divine nature in Christ was more extreme than theirs. What caused Newman alarm was not this understanding of Christ; he had no sympathy with the Monophysites. What alarmed him was the lesson the controversy suggested about the Anglican Church. He saw the extremists, the Eutychians, as Protestants. Rome, safeguarding the faith, was the same then as now. Where were the Monophysites? They were in the middle way. They may have resisted the extreme Eutychian view, but their compromising *via media* had also been condemned. "I saw my face in [a] mirror," Newman explains in his *Apologia*, "and I was a Monophysite" (*Apo.*, 114 [108]). His standpoint appeared fatally flawed. The past undid the present.

Then someone gave him an article by Nicholas Wiseman on the Anglican claim to apostolic succession. The article made little impression at first, but later a friend pointed out to him a phrase of St. Augustine's that he had passed over before, *Securus judicat orbis terrarum*. The words almost defy translation, but Newman's version was, "The universal Church is in its judgments secure of truth" (*Ess.* ii, 101). The very idea overwhelmed him. He did not, because of it, suppose that the majority was always right; sometimes the few had to withstand the many. But by those words, he later recorded, words that interpreted and summed up the long and varied course of the Anglican Church's history, "the theory of the *Via Media* was absolutely pulverized" (*Apo.*, 117 [110–111]). He felt as though he had seen a ghost, and the thought flashed through his mind, "The Church of Rome will be found right after all"; then it vanished (*Apo.*, 118 [111]).

What happened next was what happens frequently when people are busy. Newman returned to work, and the impact of his summer reading gradually faded. For two more years, there was calm. But then the ghost returned.

In 1841, while beginning again his study of fourth century Arianism, he found the earlier pattern recurring. This time it was the Arians who were like Protestants, Rome remaining the same, and the Anglican middle way, the *via media*, so far as it existed, was the path taken by the semi-Arians. Rightly or wrongly, that was how he saw it (*Apo.*, 139 [130]). And then in quick succession, two further blows fell.

Earlier in the year, he had been working on a new tract, known simply as tract No. 90. It contained his reflections on some of the Thirty-Nine Articles, the statements of Anglican doctrine established in 1563, showing how they could be interpreted in a way that was compatible with the teaching of the Council of Trent. The line, of course, was controversial. The articles were regarded by Anglicans as a bulwark against popery, Romanism, and superstition. But Newman wanted to show that, as the articles had been drawn up as part of the Elizabethan Settlement "with the purpose of including Catholics," of helping them feel at home in the Church of England, "Catholics now will not be excluded" (*V.M.* ii, 348). His motive in writing about this was to restrain some younger, headstrong Tractarians who were eager to desert the Church of England and become Roman Catholics. He anticipated trouble, but not much. He felt that people were becoming bored with Tractarianism. It was no longer attracting much attention; perhaps two or three bishops might object. He was mistaken. For the next three years, bishop after bishop condemned the tract, twenty-four of them in all. He was stunned. It was not merely the ferocity of the onslaught. Episcopal authority lay at the heart of the Tractarian understanding of the Church, obedience to it at the heart of the Tractarian disposition. Yet here were the bishops using the status he had championed for them, condemning a position he believed was inescapable. Where could he turn? He was at a loss. He could not become a Protestant. Clinging to the Church of England, reluctant to go to Rome, he wanted to follow reason, not be a victim of his emotions. Then a second blow fell, confirming the first.

A decision was taken to establish a bishopric in Jerusalem. The idea came originally from the Prussians but was supported in England by the Archbishop of Canterbury among others. It was intended to give Protestants a center in the Holy Land, and the intention was for the bishop to be alternately Anglican and Lutheran or Calvinist. Newman recoiled from the notion. He was committed to an understanding of the Church of England as distinct from Protestantism, a distinction lost on the Anglican supporters of this scheme. They were abandoning the middle way and identifying themselves as a Protestant denomination.

His patristic studies, on the one hand, and these two crises, on the other, brought Newman low. In his own words, he was "on his death-bed" as an Anglican (*Apo.*, 147 [137]), but he had not yet died. What was he to do? Where was he to go? Where was the true Church to be found? He had no faith in Protestantism, and he could no longer see the Church of England as a path between Protestant error and Roman excess. Only one possibility seemed to remain: could it be that what he had dismissed as Roman corruption was in fact evidence of authentic development? He turned increasingly, therefore, to study the theory of doctrinal development, regarding it as "a hypothesis to account for a difficulty" (*Dev.*, 30). He did not hurry. He pursued the question for four more years. Then, in due course, he gathered his findings into his *Essay on the Development of Christian Doctrine*.

The debate, detailed and particular, that his *Essay* provoked has been immense, and it still goes on. It cannot be resolved here. The drift of Newman's thought, however, may be indicated by an image and by the *Essay*'s most remembered sentence. The image is that of a stream, which he noticed, is sometimes said to be "clearest near the spring": things are purest where they begin. But then he observed: "Whatever use may fairly be made of this image, it does not apply to the history of a philosophy or belief, which on the contrary is more equable, and purer, and stronger, when its bed has become deep, and broad, and full." And he drew out his meaning at some length before concluding with the sentence that has been quoted frequently, if not always accurately: "In a higher world it is otherwise, but here below to live is to change, and to be perfect is to have changed often" (*Dev.*, 40).

He took his time over the *Essay*, but before it had been completed properly, his mind was made up. On that rainy, windswept night in October 1845, Dominic Barberi arrived, and Newman was received into the Catholic Church.

(iv)

Newman concluded his *Essay on Development* by speaking of the Catholic Church as the "Blessed Vision of Peace" (*Dev.*, 445), and it is true that in one sense his search had come to an end. There were to be no more changes like the ones we discussed already, from evangelical conversion to the prizing of intellectual excellence to Anglo-Catholicism. And in the early years, there was even a kind of honeymoon period, when he displayed at times something like the enthusiasm of a neophyte. He went to Rome to prepare for priestly ordination and was ordained as an Oratorian. He then returned to England to establish the Oratory there. The Oratorians, founded in Rome by St. Philip Neri in the sixteenth century, were secular priests who lived in community. In a way they resembled at that time the senior common room of an Oxford college. It was an ideal setting for Newman. But the honeymoon did not last. Soon he had to endure, for years, difficulties that drained him, public disgrace, obstruction, frustration, misunderstanding, and deceit. In his journal much later, written in January 1863, he remarked, "as a Protestant, I felt my religion dreary, but not my life—but, as a Catholic, my life dreary, not my religion" (*A.W.*, 254).

The public disgrace was the Achilli trial. While lecturing on Catholicism in England in 1851, Newman took the opportunity to denounce Giacinto Achilli, a former Dominican who had come to England and was attacking Catholicism on behalf of the Evangelical Alliance, an association of Protestants founded in 1846. Newman's allegations, exposing Achilli as a liar and sexual predator, merely repeated those already documented in an article by Cardinal Wiseman, so he believed he had the evidence to back his charges. But Achilli, confident that the charges could not be proved, denied them and sued for libel. Wiseman, slow and disorganized, could not find the necessary papers in time, and so the matter went to trial. One of Newman's indefatigable friends, Maria Giberne, set off for Italy to track down women whom Achilli had assaulted years previously to persuade them to come to England and give evidence on Newman's behalf. Many were now respectable wives and mothers who had no wish to relive sordid, humiliating incidents from the past, but some were persuaded to come. Nevertheless, the jury found Newman guilty, his charges considered unproven. But the trial judge, Lord Campbell, the Lord Chief Justice, was criticized for his prejudiced handling of the trial, and when the time came for sentence to be passed, Newman's counsel asked for a second trial. There was consternation. In the event, the request was denied, but instead of imprisonment, which he had expected, Newman was lectured on his own moral deterioration since becoming a Catholic and fined £100. The whole episode had hung over him for eighteen months, and although he had won a moral victory, in general he was regarded as disgraced.

While the Achilli drama was unfolding, Newman had been contacted by the Irish bishops in 1851 with a view to his becoming rector of a new Catholic university in Ireland. Newman eventually agreed and spent a great deal of time and energy on the project for the next seven years. This period was to produce his classic work *The Idea of a University*. Besides that, however, it brought him only hard labor and anxiety. In brief, there was a clash of viewpoint. While he had in mind a university reflecting the breadth of approach found at Oxford, the bishops wanted something far more limited, little more than a Catholic college. There were tensions among the bishops themselves, who were also suspicious of him; and Archbishop Paul Cullen of Dublin, who had first invited Newman to come, exasperated him, ignoring his urgent inquiries and then making decisions without informing him. Needed at his oratory in Birmingham and ground down by the obstacles that had been placed in his way, he resigned in 1858.

A further difficulty had already begun. In 1857 he was asked by the English bishops to oversee a new translation of the Bible. He felt honored. He made inquiries and drew up plans, engaging a list of contributors. He was also told that the American bishops were already engaged on a similar project. Contact with the Americans was thrown entirely on to him, and then he waited for further instructions, but after December 1858 he heard nothing more. The scheme evaporated. His efforts had been frustrated.

Then within months he was in the thick of the *Rambler* affair. The *Rambler* was a well-regarded Catholic periodical, which was at times critical of episcopal action. There were bishops who wished to censure it, and to avoid that, Newman's bishop, Ullathorne, asked him in February 1859 to persuade the editor, Richard Simpson, to resign. Then shortly afterward, Ullathorne approached him again and asked him to take on the editorship himself. Newman, although hesitant at first, eventually agreed to do so because he supported the basic purpose of the *Rambler* as a periodical for educated lay people. The idea he still advocated, however, that the laity might have something significant to contribute to the healthy life of the Church, was a step too far at that time. Visiting Newman again in May, Ullathorne now suggested he resign, even though he had scarcely begun. All the same, there was one final edition Newman was still obliged to produce, and he decided to use the opportunity to discuss the laity's role in the Church. And so he wrote his article "On Consulting the Faithful in Matters of Doctrine." It has since become renowned. But those opposed to his views attacked him in Rome. When he heard this, he sent a letter offering to show that what he had written was consistent with Church teaching, and in Rome a list of objections was drawn up for his reply. For some reason this list, entrusted to Cardinal Wiseman, was never passed on to him. As he heard nothing, he thought the matter had been dropped, while Rome assumed he was unwilling to answer. Misunderstanding bred suspicion, and he remained under scrutiny in Rome for the next eight years. Only when some friends visited the Vatican in 1867 was the matter finally clarified and resolved.

Constant adversity, blow after blow, public disgrace, episcopal obstruction, frustration, and misunderstanding reduced him to silence. By 1863 he was at a low point. Throughout his life he had tried to follow the truth wherever it had led him, at whatever cost, and he had suffered for it. And then he was attacked again. Just before the New Year, he was sent a copy of *Macmillan's Magazine* for January 1864. In a book review, Charles Kingsley, Anglican clergyman, professor of modern history at Cambridge, and novelist, remarked in passing,

> Truth, for its own sake, had never been a virtue with the Roman clergy. Father Newman informs us that it need not, and on the whole ought not to be; that cunning is the weapon which heaven has given to the Saints wherewith to withstand the brute male force of the wicked world which marries and is given in marriage. Whether his notion be doctrinally correct or not, it is at least historically so.

Newman stirred. Letters were exchanged with *Macmillan's* publisher and with Kingsley, but he found them unsatisfactory. He realized that the answer to the charge laid against him would never come from controversy alone, a trading of arguments. In any case, it was his truthfulness, his handling of arguments, that was under attack. So he decided to set out the history of his religious opinions. This was his *Apologia pro Vita Sua*. People need not agree with him or be persuaded by the views he held, but at least they might come to see that he had behaved with integrity and held his views honestly. And, moreover, in giving his account, he was able to pay tribute to old friends, to acknowledge what he owed them, and to express his enduring affection for them. What he wrote, reliving the sorrows and separations of the past, caused him acute pain, but it was received and welcomed warmly almost without exception. After nearly twenty years, many friendships were restored, his gifts came to be recognized, and his influence once more began to grow.

All the same, there were further hardships to be faced. The most obvious difficulty revolved around the plan for him to establish an Oratorian mission in Oxford. Many English Catholics supported the idea. They wanted their sons to go up to the university in spite of the disapproval of Church authorities, and they regarded Newman as the ideal person to be there to give them pastoral care. Bishop Ullathorne also supported the initiative. Newman obeyed his bishop and started to plan, finding a site, raising money. But those Catholics who opposed the idea, because they regarded Oxford as anti-Catholic, were fiercely opposed to Newman's presence. They feared that once he was there, he would act like a magnet, and even more of the young would be attracted to the university. These opponents, notably Henry Manning, the new Archbishop of Westminster, who had once been his friend, were influential, especially in Rome. And so a condition for establishing the oratory was laid down but hidden from Newman: Newman himself was not permitted to reside. When it leaked out and the outcome became clear, Newman wrote to Ullathorne with regret and withdrew from the mission. The plan was over. Accepting his decision, Ullathorne replied with sadness that he had been "shamefully misrepresented at Rome, and that by countrymen of our own" (*L.D.* xxiii, 312, n.2). He was the victim of deceit.

Other controversies followed, notably with Pusey and through the debates that arose around the definition of papal infallibility. Once more, he clashed with Manning, who had adopted an extreme ultramontane line. Nevertheless, amid the stress of controversy, there was also a triumph. In 1870, Newman managed at last to publish his *Essay in Aid of a Grammar of Assent.*

(*v*)

Those who know only one thing about Newman, that he made a distinction between real and notional assent, will find that distinction explained here: in general, notional assents are intellectual and abstract and do not affect our conduct, while real assent is concerned with what is concrete and stirs us to action (*G.A.*, 89–91 [63–64]). Besides that, his *Essay in Aid of a Grammar of Assent* is unique among Newman's works as the only one that was not occasional, in the sense of being triggered by a particular occasion or need; it was prompted rather by his lifelong desire to respond to a specific pastoral concern, to show that religious faith was rational, that it was reasonable to believe. He had expressed sharply the objection he wanted to refute in an exploratory paper in 1860:

> The great mass of Catholics know nothing of argument; how then is their faith rational? The peasant believes "what he is told," and if his priest told him the Holy Ghost was incarnate, he would have faith in that heresy. Catholics are forbidden to reconsider the truth of their faith.[4]

That was the problem he wanted to tackle, but the *Grammar*, for all its elegance, was not immediately easy to understand. Fortunately for us, however, Newman had a conversation with his friend and fellow Oratorian Edward Caswall seven years after the book was published, in 1877, and Caswall made a note of what he had told him on the flyleaf of his copy. "Object of the book twofold," Caswall wrote. "In the first part shows that you can believe what you cannot understand. In the second part that you can believe what you cannot absolutely prove."[5] But even this note needs to be explained.

When Newman observed that you can believe what you cannot understand, he was not discounting understanding as superfluous or unnecessary; he meant rather that belief does not depend upon understanding. There is a distinction between them. What we may come to understand through the cool processes of abstract reasoning may indeed convince us, but without moving us to believe. Belief is a different state of mind. It is personal. When we believe, he declared, "Persons influence us, voices melt us, looks subdue us, deeds inflame us." We do not make sacrifices for abstractions: "no man will be a martyr for a conclusion"; but many people give their lives for what they believe: they will "live and die upon a dogma" (*G.A.*, 93 [66]).

And as belief does not depend upon understanding, neither does it depend upon absolute proof. This was the second position Newman wished to establish. He wanted to show that the kind of proof that undergirds belief is not absolute according to some strict, formal demonstration but is often made up of an accumulation or convergence of probabilities. His clearest image was not used in the *Grammar* but appeared in a letter to one of his regular correspondents, Canon John Walker, on July 6, 1864. He likened the certitude supplied by absolute proof to an iron rod and the certitude that supports belief to "a *cable* which is made up of a number of separate threads, each feeble," yet which, when woven together, are unbreakable (*L.D.* xxi, 146). I suspect that many people can recognize what he meant and agree. An obvious example for me, as rector of a seminary, occurs whenever I have to recommend someone for ordination. Have I absolute proof that the person is suitable? Of course not; I could be mistaken. But when over a significant period of time I find a pattern emerging of fidelity to prayer, intellectual competence, and pastoral commitment, all well integrated within a mature human personality, I feel able with confidence to make my recommendation. None of these elements—spiritual, intellectual, pastoral, and human— taken singly, can ensure fitness for ordination, but together they combine to create certitude. And we discover that certitude by using what Newman called in the *Grammar* our illative sense, which he described as "a grand word for an common thing" (*L.D.* xxiv, 375).

Illation is reasoning. The illative sense, therefore, refers to the human capacity for reasoning, our gift for assessing evidence and, Newman claimed, doing so accurately. Inadequate evidence, of course, will mislead us, but given the evidence, as Newman had stated many years before, we commonly reason well (*U.S.*, 211). This confidence in the human condition was fundamental for him. When using our illative sense, we weigh the evidence, discern the patterns in the converging probabilities, and come to certitude. Moreover, for him, the process was always intensely personal. As we noticed earlier, toward the end of the *Grammar*, he declared, "I say plainly I do not want to be converted by a smart syllogism; if I am asked to convert others by it, I say plainly I do not care to overcome their reason without touching their hearts" (*G.A.*, 425 [273]).

A Grammar of Assent was perhaps his crowning literary achievement. And then in 1879 there came a great surprise.

(vi)

Pope Leo XIII, who had succeeded Pius IX in 1878, planned to create new cardinals, and among them, he hoped, would be Newman. It was a gracious gesture, but even so there was drama. Cardinals who were not diocesan bishops usually resided in Rome. When Newman was approached and told of the pope's wish, he was deeply grateful for the honor that would be done him and wanted to accept, but for him to leave Birmingham at his age—he was seventy-eight—was, he felt, impossible. All the same, he did not wish even to seem to be bargaining, putting terms on his acceptance to the pope. He discussed his dilemma with Ullathorne, who had brought him the news. Ullathorne advised him to write a letter to the pope, which Newman did, expressing his gratitude to him and also his desire to remain in his "much loved Oratory" (*L.D.* xxix, 19). Ullathorne then added a letter of his own to accompany Newman's, explaining clearly Newman's wish to accept but his reluctance to leave Birmingham, which, he added, he was sure was never "the Holy Father's intention" (*L.D.* xxix, 20). He then sent these two letters to Cardinal Manning, who was due to leave for Rome and deliver them. But Manning forwarded only Newman's letter without Ullathorne's explanation, so that the desire he expressed to remain in Birmingham seemed like a refusal of the honor. He also let slip the news that Newman had refused. When that became known, there was an outcry. All kinds of people protested. And Newman's answer to inquirers who wanted to know the reason for his refusal was plain: he could not refuse an offer he had yet to receive; no formal invitation had been made. Manning, realizing his blunder, went quickly to the pope to put the matter right. Then the formal news of Newman's elevation was sent to Birmingham, and he received his cardinal's hat in Rome on May 15, 1879. The cloud, as he said, had been lifted from him forever. He lived for a further eleven years, dying in 1890. He was eighty-nine.

(vii)

Newman's long life was obviously far fuller and more complex than this account can convey. His personality and ideas, as well as the interpretation placed on events, have led to a whole industry of Newman studies and scholarship. His genius is original and farsighted, constantly breaking new ground. There are those whose admiration for Newman makes them believe he could do no wrong. Admiring Newman, as I do, and conscious of my debt to him, that is nevertheless not the attitude that I feel needs to be adopted here. There can always be alternative views. Newman does not win over everyone. Some find him personally too sensitive, or too ruthless in argument, or too determined always to be right. Let it be so.

All this account has tried to do is describe the path he pursued throughout his life, showing that he tried to follow it consistently and honestly. First, he was led from evangelicalism through rationalism to Anglicanism and then on to Catholicism; after that, once a Catholic, holding to the same path, he endured trials and humiliation, until unexpectedly Pope Leo XIII honored him as a cardinal. At his death, as he declared, according to the epitaph he himself had composed, he passed out of the shadows and images into the truth: *ex umbris et imaginibus in veritatem.* That had been his desired destination all along.

3

A Mind Alive

(i)

However difficult it may be to chart the course of Newman's long and involved life, it is still more demanding to capture the character of his mind. One reason for that is something personal, something about him. It was identified neatly by Catholic theologian Nicholas Lash when he drew attention to "that very *closeness* of speech to speaker, of text to thinker, which is the hallmark of his genius."[1] Sometimes people have written about Newman's theological method and even done it rather well. Nevertheless, the theories they parade can seem stiff and alien because, as Lash explains, "it is *Newman* who makes the difference to those touched by his spell, far more than his arguments or ideas considered in abstraction."[2] While mapping the mind, we must never forget the man.

The man was always more interested in reality than theory. He was concerned with what actually happened. His sympathies lay instinctively with a process of reasoning that was direct and immediate. So in 1870, in his *Grammar of Assent*, he declared: "I say, then, that our most natural mode of reasoning is, not from propositions to propositions, but from things to things, from concrete to concrete, from wholes to wholes" (*G.A.*, 330 [213–214]). That was his style, and we notice at once the way this approach is naturally in tune with the priority he gave to pastoral care throughout his life. There will be other examples.

Besides that, when reading Newman, we may also become aware of certain preoccupations that appear time after time. There are themes that give unity to his life and way of thinking. First, there was his devotion to the cause of revealed religion. Toward the end of his life, in 1877, he stated, "Revelation is the initial and essential idea of Christianity" (*V.M.* i, xlvii [29]). Stephen Dessain believed that this cause was the fundamental interest of his life.[3] Next, there was his search for the Church, which we have considered already. What has been revealed, be it ever so pregnant with meaning, is void unless received. Faith receives the revelation, but faith is never disembodied. To be more precise, it is the Church, as the community of faith, that receives and seeks to live the revelation. Church and revelation are inseparably linked.

Revelation, of course, is made known in a particularly privileged way through sacred scripture, but it is found there, as Newman used to say, unsystematically (*Ari.*, 147). Consequently later, under the pressure of controversy, what has been received through scripture needs to be given sharper focus. And so his third preoccupation was with dogma, the interpreting and distilling of what has been revealed. "From the age of fifteen," he remarked in his *Apologia*, "dogma has been the fundamental principle of my religion" (*Apo.*, 49 [54]). And what has been revealed, and received by the Church, and articulated as dogma, is meant also to be communicated. And so the fourth key preoccupation of Newman's life was with education, the need to provide people with a deeper understanding of their faith so that they might be better able to give an account of it. In his journal in January 1863, when at a low point in his life, he recorded, "from first to last, education, in this large sense of the word, has been my line" (*A.W.*, 259).

To note these four themes—revelation, the Church, dogma, and education—as well as the relationship among them, should not, however, mislead anyone into shaping a theory of Newman's thought in their terms. They are noteworthy simply because they recur in his writings like refrains.

Nevertheless, the question remains. How can we capture the character of Newman's mind, the tenor of his thinking? How is it best to proceed? One occasion that happened late in his life may be a good place to start.

(ii)

On May 12, 1879, Newman was waiting with his friends and others who were in attendance at the Palazzo della Pigna in Rome. The misunderstanding surrounding his acceptance of the invitation to become a cardinal had been resolved. And then at eleven o'clock that morning, Cardinal Lorenzo Nina, the Secretary of State, arrived from the Vatican, bringing a brief letter, a *biglietto*, from Pope Leo XIII to inform Newman that he had that morning been made a cardinal. Newman thanked him and then made a speech, which has since become famous. In it he declared: "I rejoice to say, to one great mischief I have from the first opposed myself. For thirty, forty, fifty years I have resisted to the best of my powers the spirit of Liberalism in religion." Now, liberalism is an elusive concept. For some it is admirable because it breathes a spirit of tolerance, a lack of coercion, while for others it does harm because it is vague and ill-defined, an invitation to relativism. Newman himself was happy to praise its virtues such as justice and truthfulness—he did so later in this very speech—but here more specifically he was concerned with liberalism in religion, and his view seems clear. He went on:

> Liberalism in religion is the doctrine that there is no positive truth in religion, but that one creed is as good as another. . . . It is inconsistent with any recognition of any religion, as *true*. It teaches that all are to be tolerated, for all are matters of

> opinion. Revealed religion is not a truth, but a sentiment and a taste; not an objective fact, not miraculous; and it is the right of each individual to make it say just what strikes his fancy.[4]

These words have sometimes led to the claim that Newman was simply "against the liberals." But the truth is subtler and more interesting. He was responding to circumstances. That does not mean he was merely being subjective himself; rather, he was reacting to the situation confronting him.

As an Anglican championing dogma, Newman opposed those who had come to regard creeds, in his words, as "fetters on souls" (*P.S.* ii, 261) and dismissed the great controversies about the Trinity and the Christ that had racked the Church in the early centuries as "the strict and technical niceties of doctrine" (*P.S.* ii, 166–167). That attitude appalled him. Expressed in those terms, it may seem to us obscure and theoretical. For Newman, however, it was immediate and exemplified in particular by the views of Renn Dickson Hampden.

Newman and Hampden

Hampden was the principal of St. Mary Hall, one of the lesser Oxford halls at the time, who was appointed Regius Professor of Divinity at Oxford in 1836. He has been described as "by nature a scholar; a learned man of no charisma and little charm."[5] His appointment, however, was controversial on both political and theological grounds. There were those who rejoiced at the opportunity it gave them to embarrass Prime Minister Lord Melbourne's government: charges against Hampden's orthodoxy made it possible to present his status as a Whig as an attack on the faith of the Anglican Church. Others resented his selection because he favored the admission of dissenters to the university and by doing so seemed to threaten that bastion of Anglican orthodoxy. And a few, particularly Newman and his friends, were convinced that his writings were heretical and that he was, therefore, unfit for the post in any case. Scholars are still divided over the dispute. It is not possible or necessary to settle the issues here. Newman scholar David Newsome's words seem characteristically well judged. "In retrospect," he observes, "it is difficult to resist the conclusion that everyone involved in these proceedings behaved rather badly."[6] Our concerns are more specific.

What roused Newman was the distinction Hampden made between the divine facts, as he called them, which are revealed in the scriptures, and everything else. Everything else, even the creeds proclaimed by Councils in Nicaea and Chalcedon, was, he affirmed, merely human speculation. In his pamphlet in support of dissenters being admitted to Oxford, a pamphlet that includes much good sense, he used as an example what he called "the extreme case of the Unitarians." Even they, he declared, had received both the Old and New Testaments and by doing so, in his view, had accepted the whole basis of revelation. What they rejected or explained away, he argued, was by virtue of that explanation, not self-evident, revealed fact but rather part of human speculation.[7] This was the distinction that stirred Newman to protest.

When the controversy about Hampden's appointment was at its height, he sat up overnight and wrote a pamphlet reviewing and criticizing Hampden's position. It was called *Elucidations of Dr. Hampden's Theological Statements* and consisted of quotations from Hampden's writings interspersed with comments of his own. He treated Hampden roughly, even, many would say, unjustly, but his purpose in the pamphlet was not to offer a poised critique of Hampden's thought but rather, as he explained soon afterward, to suggest "bases for an examination of [his] opinion" (*L.D.* v, 233). And on February 14, he left a copy of the pamphlet at Hampden's door.

Hampden acknowledged it immediately and graciously. But his eye had been caught by one statement in particular. "I am shocked," he observed,

> to find it attributed to me that I do not hold the
> truths of the Trinity and the Incarnation as "re-
> vealed"; God forbid, I solemnly say, that ever such
> a thought should have crossed my mind, or have

been really conveyed to any one by an inadver-
tence of expression on my part.[8]

He demanded a retraction in the most explicit terms. Newman
replied at once, and his reply brings us to the heart of the issue.

He explained to Hampden that he was concerned with his
writings, not his personal beliefs. He told him: "I hope I am duly
impressed by your serious protestation of your belief in the Trinity and Incarnation, and beg to remind you, I have no where expressed a doubt of it." Then he went on:

> I have spoken of you only as an author, and, *as
> such*, you seem to lie open to my remark, for since
> you state in your pamphlet that an Unitarian
> holds "the *whole* revelation" *as holding* "the basis
> of divine facts", you surely do deny that "the truths
> of the Trinity and the Incarnation" are "revealed."
> (*L.D.* v, 235–236)

In other words, Newman was arguing, if Unitarians, because they
accept the Bible, are Christians, although they reject the Trinity
and the Incarnation, how can these beliefs be upheld as revealed
and essential to Christianity? That was his point. Hampden appealed indeed to revelation, but his understanding of revelation
was so restricted that later formulations of dogma were in his view
merely matters of truths of opinion. They could have no higher
status. What was revealed was in the Bible and obvious, evident
because beyond dispute, what had emerged later through controversy, having failed that criterion, could not claim the same status.
It could be only speculation. And that was the viewpoint Newman
attacked.

For him, as we have seen, scripture was unsystematic. Had
disputes over its interpretation not arisen, it alone would have
been enough; in fact, he thought, that would have been the ideal.
But it was not to be. Human reality is more complex. People argue. Interpretations of what had been revealed were disputed, but
what had then been hammered out in controversy and defined in
creeds and dogmas could not for that reason be regarded as mere

speculation or a matter of opinion. When particular theological opinions came in due course to be canonized in creeds and dogmas, they acquired by that very fact a higher status.

Newman explained his position in his final University Sermon in 1843, when he declared: "Creeds and dogmas live in the one idea which they are designed to express, and which alone is substantive; . . . the Catholic dogmas are, after all, but symbols of a Divine fact" (*U.S.*, 331–332). They symbolize the revealed truths they express. And the reference to symbols is telling, for Newman was writing within the literary tradition of Romantic poets like Coleridge and Wordsworth. As Stephen Prickett, former Regius Professor of English Literature at Glasgow University, has noted, "Anyone who has read both literary criticism and theology in the Victorian period soon comes to realize how deeply the two are intertwined."[9] Within that tradition symbols were not arbitrary, external tokens of what they express; "form and content were essentially indivisible"; symbols were a part of, and shared in, the reality they symbolized. "It was not possible to describe the 'meaning' of the *Ancient Mariner* in other terms than those of the poem."[10] They had a kind of sacramental quality. That was the tradition within which Newman was working. Accordingly, dogma was privileged. It was not arbitrary, one possible expression of teaching among many. It had special status. It articulated what has been revealed and was wedded to it indissolubly.[11]

There is much more that could be said. It is not necessary to resolve the dispute between Newman and Hampden here. This, however, may be enough to illustrate, from Newman's Anglican years, his claim in 1879. Whatever the merits of Hampden's standpoint, Newman saw himself as resisting the spirit of liberalism in religion, defending dogma against a view that would reduce it to human speculation, something not binding, a fancy a person might take or leave.

Newman and Ward

After Newman had become a Catholic in 1845, his theological work had much in common with the work of his Anglican period. There were sermons rich in theological content, detailed patristic studies, and the same abiding interest in the relationship between faith and reason. Nor had his commitment to dogma changed. But his circumstances had. For the Anglican Newman, as we have seen, the dogmatic principle had priority and needed to be safeguarded, but as a Catholic, the scene was different. In the Catholic Church, dogma was not at risk; rather the contrary, it was in the ascendant. And in the ascendant with it was a dogmatizing spirit, narrow, rigid, and authoritarian, aggressive, unimaginative, and hostile to alternatives. Those with that cast of mind found it hard, if not impossible, not to canonize their own opinions as definitive and condemn any alternative as unsound. If his dispute with Hampden can be said to illustrate Newman's attitude and approach during his Anglican years, then his relationship with W.G. Ward may do the same while he was a Catholic.

W.G. Ward was a gifted, pure mathematician. It is perhaps significant that he could not bear applied mathematics. He delighted in pushing arguments to their logical conclusion, and that approach marked his theology as well. As a young man at Oxford, he had at first taken no interest in the Tractarians. Urged to hear Newman preach, he had dismissed the notion out of hand: "Why should I go and listen to such myths?"[12] he asked. But later he went, and once he had done so, his life was changed. He became at first one of Newman's most enthusiastic followers.

Ward's enthusiasm led him to be received into the Catholic Church before Newman. He became an extreme ultramontane. He is famous for wishing to have "a new papal Bull every morning with my *Times* at breakfast," although people usually fail to recognize the paradoxical humor underlying the remark.[13] Ward was an engaging character, blessed with a keen sense of humor. I particularly enjoy the story of when he went to the theater on King William Street. The theater itself had previously been the home of the London Oratorians before they moved to Brompton with Frederick Faber as their superior. Faber was another warm-hearted enthusiast who had been a disciple of Newman's and also tended to extremism. He and Newman were to clash bitterly. Faber was

Ward's spiritual director. On this occasion, however, sitting in the theater between acts, Ward was struck by two thoughts. "The first," he later admitted to Faber, "was, Last time I was in this building I heard Faber preach. The second was, How much more I am enjoying myself tonight than I did the last time I was here"[14]

Ward always retained an affection for Newman despite their differences. Years later he told him that those differences made him feel like "a kind of intellectual orphan."[15] Newman for his part remained fond of Ward; nevertheless, he became exasperated by Ward's dogmatizing spirit, the way he exaggerated devotion to Mary and advocated an extreme view of papal authority. We shall come across examples later.

He also became weary of Ward's confidence in his own opinions, his tendency to regard even minor differences as matters of great importance. He described their relationship adroitly in a letter in 1862. Ward asked if he could pay him a visit, and Newman replied, welcoming him. But he then sketched how he foresaw the pattern of their conversation.

> If things are to go as they have gone, I should anticipate our conversation would have this result: viz, you would begin by stating that I hold something very different from, or the reverse of, what I really hold. I should undeceive you, and you would confess that you were mistaken. Then we should branch off to some independent subject of theology, and you would be pleased to find that I agreed with you, when others did not. You would leave—and then, in a few weeks, you would write me word, that it pained you bitterly to think that we were diverging from each other in theological opinion more and more. If I then wrote to inquire what you could mean, you would answer that you really could not at the moment recollect the grounds on which you had been led to say so; but you would not withdraw it.

> Thus I have to endure, in spite of your real affection for me, a never-dying misgiving on your part that I am in some substantial matter at variance with you—while I for my part sincerely think that on *no* subject is there any substantial difference between us, as far as theology is concerned. (*L.D.* xx, 191)

That final phrase, "as far as theology is concerned," is revealing because it points to a situation that Ward's position and cast of mind found it hard to allow: the legitimate coexistence of differing points of view. He never learned the lesson Newman had tried to teach him earlier, "to bear and forbear" (*L.D.* xvi, 486). That was Newman's standpoint, his priority as a Catholic, where dogma was secure but theology under threat. He always prized dogma, but as a Catholic he championed freedom in theology as well because he was aware of the threat posed by dogmatic fundamentalism.

(iii)

Newman's appreciation of theology was expressed most precisely in 1877, when he called it "the fundamental and regulating principle of the whole Church system" (*V.M.* i, xlvii [29]). He was preparing his *Lectures on the Prophetical Office of the Church* for inclusion in the uniform edition of his works. He did not wish to alter the text he had prepared forty years earlier, but the changes in his views from the time when he wrote this book, at the peak of his influence as an Anglican, to this time, when he had been a Catholic for more than thirty years, were so great that it called for something more than explanatory footnotes. He decided, therefore, to write a special preface for this new edition. In it he reflected not only on the prophetical office of the original title but on the priestly and kingly offices as well; and indeed he considered their relationships to one another. It was while discussing these three offices that he spoke of theology as the fundamental and regulating principle. He called it that because he regarded it as "commensurate with Revelation," and he called revelation "the initial and essential idea of Christianity." And from revelation and its theology, he went on to argue, priesthood and kingship flow (*V.M.* i, xlvii [29]). All the same, nowadays the attention given to the offices may seem rather static. Some time after the new edition, Baron Friedrich von Hügel took up the idea in more dynamic terms.

Von Hügel did not concentrate on the offices so much as the adjectives that go with them: kings lead institutions and so are concerned with what is institutional; prophets teach and so are concerned with what is intellectual; and priests, celebrating the mysteries, should be devoted to the mystical.[16] And so we shift from the titles king, prophet, and priest to the qualities they imply, the institutional, the intellectual, and the mystical. By doing so, we also come to recognize more readily the virtues that go with those qualities: what is institutional demands loyalty, what is intellectual prompts questioning, while what is mystical invites contemplation. And these qualities and their virtues are not static. They grow, develop, mature. And while they need to be interwoven as constant elements in our lives, each has a time when it commands priority.

Loyalty is, first of all, a characteristic of children. What we first encounter, our earliest experiences, we take to be normal at the start and guard loyally. Later, as adolescents, we discover that life is not so simple, and we find ourselves stirred to ask a range of questions. Then, as we move into maturity, the perspective changes again: we are led on to gaze, to contemplate. It is not a matter of moving distinctly and cleanly from one phase to the next. They are not independent compartments. Each quality is to be valued and maintained, and they need to be integrated. When those who are loyal confront questions, they do not, therefore, become disloyal; rather, their loyalty is refined. And as they move into contemplation, they may still wrestle with questions, but the struggle has changed character, become less anxious, more tranquil.

What makes this approach particularly significant here, however, is the part played by questioning—in this context, by theology. Newman called it fundamental and regulating, and it is possible to see why. He was not making what is rational supreme but recognizing it instead as the hinge for our development. Understanding, intellectual activity, challenges our initial loyalties, checks our prejudices, and frees us from our rigid, preconceived ideas. And then, as we explore it and discover its limitations, we find ourselves being ushered into a place beyond intellectual achievement alone, where we gaze, contemplate, and plumb still greater depths. Theology is the regulating hinge. It matures our loyalty and launches us into contemplation.

Newman's commitment to dogma was never obscurantist, a refusal to face questioning. He valued theology; he regarded its role as indispensable. But, returning to his speech in 1879, the question may still be raised: if, during his Catholic years, his approach to theology was sound and dogma was secure, in what sense could he be said to have been actively resisting religious liberalism? Yet, in fact, he had. But the target was not so much anti-dogmatic Christian believers; rather, it was what he called "a darkness different in kind from any that has been before it."[17]

(iv)

The phrase came from a sermon he preached in 1873 that was called "The Infidelity of the Future." Newman looked ahead and tried to describe the kind of society that he foresaw developing and in which the Catholic Church must live. Many details ring true today in the Western world: the waning influence of other Christian communities; the resistance to Catholicism, particularly when its influence is felt to grow; the setbacks created by scandals; the problems that arise from shallow thinking in what we might call media culture, for, in Newman's words, "a fool may ask a hundred questions which a wise man cannot answer"; and the genuine difficulties that there are in revealed religion in any case. But the root cause of these concerns he identified in a single sentence: "Christianity has never yet had experience of a world simply irreligious."[18] Is this prediction too bleak? Not obviously.

In Western society today, as we know, personal freedom is so cherished that nothing must be allowed to threaten it, but that is what revealed religion's claim of objective truth appears to do. Objective truth, wherever found, would have to take priority over everything else. In Western eyes, that cannot be permitted. Personal freedom must never be restrained. What is possible is in general assumed to be permissible, in relationships, in science, in medicine, in professional or political life. We test the limits like adolescents, often insensitive to a moral or ethical dimension. In any case, we ask: what is truth?

The concept of "objective truth" is, of course, a difficult one. Western society may once have defended it, but the critique has kept moving, dissolving confidence in coherence, in finding meaning, and in commitment. The narrative has collapsed. Here is the fragmentation known as post-modernism. Viewpoints shatter and relationships break down. Where are we to turn? In such a landscape, confused, fragmented, uncommitted, Western society argues that only the personal, the subjective, the relative are secure. It is in many respects the scene Newman foresaw, a view of the world in which religion has no place.

Someone else who recognized this was Pope Benedict XVI. Preaching to the College of Cardinals on April 18, 2005, at the Mass before they entered the conclave from which he was to emerge as pope, he used the image of the Church as a boat, tossed on the waves created by ideological currents, "from Marxism to liberalism, even to libertinism; from collectivism to radical individualism; from atheism to a vague religious mysticism; from agnosticism to syncretism and so forth." He was regarded at the time as excessively pessimistic, particularly when he concluded, "We are building a dictatorship of relativism that does not recognize anything as definitive and whose ultimate goal consists solely of one's own ego and desires."[19] His phrase "the dictatorship of relativism" may seem severe, and yet it can be linked to Newman's "a world simply irreligious." And the connection is not necessarily a coincidence.

For Pope Benedict, relativism was a threat because when we abandon objective truth, it is not that nothing is true, but that anything can be true. And it gets worse. For where there are no criteria to safeguard truth, you do not have tolerance; you have whatever truth those in power decide it should be. Freedom divorced from truth will not be protected; it will be lost. When we abandon truth, we abandon freedom as well. And so the pope has spoken of the abandonment of objective truth as a slide into totalitarianism, placing us at the mercy of a dictator. The reference to totalitarianism may seem emotive and extreme, but we should remember that Benedict has experience of what he is saying.[20]

He has addressed the issue on a number of occasions, but one that is particularly notable here was a conference held in Rome in 1990 to mark the one hundred–year anniversary of Newman's death. On that occasion he referred to the bond between truth and personal conscience.

As Cardinal Joseph Ratzinger, he spoke first about his own introduction to Newman's thought when he was a young seminarian shortly after the Second World War. He went on to stress at once the importance for him of Newman's teaching on conscience. Newman taught that conscience was to be cherished, he explained, as "a way of obedience to objective truth." And Newman's whole life bore witness to that conviction. The future pope's earlier experience, however, had been very different. "We had experienced," he told the conference, "the claim of a totalitarian party which understood itself as the fulfillment of history and which negated the conscience of the individual. One of its leaders [Hermann Goering] had said: 'I have no conscience. My conscience is Adolf Hitler.'"[21] Here is the slide into totalitarianism. When truth is disregarded, when there is no objective standard to which we can appeal, we do not create space for easy tolerance. Instead, freedom is left defenseless, at the mercy of those in power. The young Joseph Ratzinger experienced what Newman had at least implicitly predicted, the consequences when revealed religion is not recognized as true, as objective, but is regarded as something private from which people may select for themselves whatever they please.

(v)

There is, of course, far more to the pattern of Newman's thought than this brief account can indicate. Other aspects will emerge as we proceed, but his speech in Rome in 1879 when he was made a cardinal at least offers us a perspective. His opposition to religious liberalism and his commitment to the dogmatic principle shaped his approach throughout his life, whether he was in controversy with those indifferent to dogma in his early Anglican days or working to overcome the narrower dogmatizing spirit he discovered later among Catholics. In both instances he was inspired by the same principle.

The dovetailing of his view on religious liberalism with the position adopted by Pope Benedict XVI, a position possibly influenced by Newman's own standpoint, suggests the next step we should take. In 1870, the Catholic teaching on papal infallibility was defined as a dogma. The definition delighted some and distressed others. There was controversy beforehand and debate afterward. Newman found himself drawn into the fray. His position has often been regarded as significant, offering a wise interpretation of what was declared.

4

Infallible Authority

(i)

In 1967 Pope Paul VI made a statement that startled many people. Addressing the Secretariat for Promoting Christian Unity on April 28 that year, he declared: "The Pope, as we well know, is undoubtedly the gravest obstacle in the path of ecumenism."[1] And Pope John Paul II was in a way echoing the same sentiment in his encyclical *May They Be One* when he acknowledged that papal primacy, which should have been a service, "sometimes manifested itself in a very different light" (*Ut Unum Sint*, no. 95). Both men were recognizing the difficulty people have had understanding the nature of papal ministry. And this difficulty has been felt not only by those outside the Catholic Church; some of those within it have also been critical. Father Hans Küng is the obvious example with his book *Infallible?*, published in 1970 to coincide with the centenary of the formal definition of papal infallibility at the First Vatican Council.

Küng felt impelled to write because he believed that the legacy of Pope John XXIII and the Second Vatican Council was being squandered by the way in which Paul VI was exercising his papal ministry. The Council's emphasis on dialogue and consultation was, he argued, being ignored in favor of the old absolutist style. He praised the pope's good intentions but was dismayed by his decisions about priestly celibacy and contraception and by his tendency to accord certain Roman theological opinions a status he felt they did not deserve. So many years later it makes no sense to try to settle those specific issues here. They still arouse debate, but the scene Küng described has shifted. The tension now is seen rather to lie between restoration and renewal. All the same, Küng's fundamental concern remains significant. "Even when the Church's claim to infallibility is not explicit," he remarked, "it is always subliminally present."[2] What makes it noteworthy is the way it dovetails with concerns expressed one hundred years earlier.

During the preparations for the First Vatican Council, when the desire developed for papal infallibility to be defined formally as a dogma of the Church, some people opposed it. They did not do so in general because they denied the teaching but because they feared too extravagant a definition. It was a difficult time.

Among the bishops who favored the definition, however, and championed it, one of the most prominent was Henry Manning, the Archbishop of Westminster. His relationship with Newman had once been warm but had become much cooler. And after the Council, Manning wrote a long pastoral letter to the priests of his diocese to introduce and explain what had been defined. In it he included within the purview of the infallible authority of the pope "the whole revealed order of salvation," such matters as "Things which pertain to faith," "Things pertaining to piety," "Things of religion," "Things of faith speculative and practical," and "Controversies of religion."[3] The very looseness of language was liable to arouse suspicion. Where were the limits? Manning's approach seemed to be sowing the seeds of what has come to be called "creeping infallibility," an exercise of infallible authority that seems at first to grow so gradually it is hardly noticed but then could run out of control. What delighted him made others anxious. And those who were anxious often turned to Newman.

Some years later, when he was drawn into the controversy more publicly, Newman was to observe that the frustrations felt by many had often been caused by Catholics themselves. He was critical of extreme enthusiasts. For years, he wrote, there have been those who

> have conducted themselves as if no responsibility attached to wild words and overbearing deeds; who have stated truths in the most paradoxical form, and stretched principles till they were close upon snapping; and who at length, having done their best to set the house on fire, leave to others the task of putting out the flame. (*Diff.* ii, 176–177)

By that time he had been fighting such fires for years.

(ii)

As we have seen, the Anglican Newman regarded infallibility, if it existed at all, as a characteristic of the undivided Church. Since, as he then believed, the Church Catholic had split into several branches, Roman, Eastern, and Anglican, it had forfeited that gift. He put it starkly: ". . . since the Church is now not one, it is not infallible; . . . the full prophetical idea is not now fulfilled" (*V.M.* i, 201 [228]). He preferred to speak of indefectibility, the confidence that the Church would not fail.

As he moved toward the Catholic Church, however, he rejected this branch theory of the Church. Moreover, as he reflected more deeply on the nature of Christianity as revelation and indeed as a revelation whose depths become known gradually through development, so he became convinced of the presence in the Church of infallibility as that necessary gift that is able to recognize and guarantee the truth of the teaching that emerged. He acknowledged the distinction between a revelation and its guarantee as true; the one did not inevitably imply the other: a revelation did not have to be guaranteed. All the same, he argued that Christianity is different because it comes precisely as a revelation, "as a whole, objectively, and with a profession of infallibility" (*Dev.*, 79–80).

Arguments about infallibility continued. Newman set out his own understanding in various places, notably in his *Essay on Development* and his *Apologia*. The point to recognize here is that he was himself convinced of it independently of the teaching of the First Vatican Council. It was not something about which he had doubts, but felt forced to accept once the pope in Council had proclaimed the definition. Nonetheless, he had not been a supporter of the definition as such. On September 20, 1869, he made a rough note and asked himself a question: "Why is it, if I believe the Pope's Infallibility I do not wish it defined?" And he replied, "I answer, because it can't be so defined as not to raise more questions than it solves" (*L.D.* xxiv, 334, n.2). It was the possible terms of the definition that worried him.

During the Council, as he became aware of the vigor with which those who favored the definition were pursuing their objective, his anxiety grew and he became indignant. On January 28, 1870, he wrote a private letter to his own bishop, William Ullathorne. In it he criticized the desire to define papal infallibility as unnecessary because people in practice believed it in any case; a definition, he wrote, would be "thunder in the clear sky, and we are told to prepare for something we know not what to try our faith we know not how." He also criticized the move as unhistorical. "When has definition of doctrine de fide been a luxury of devotion," he asked, "and not a stern painful necessity?" And he denounced the "aggressive insolent faction . . . [who] 'make the heart of the just to mourn, whom the Lord hath not made sorrowful'" (*L.D.* xxv, 18–19). It was not an isolated protest.

On August 21 in the same year, he wrote to his friend Ambrose St. John and referred to "the tyrant majority." He advised a policy of perfect quiet, in case it "should do something more" (*L.D.* xxv, 192). But perhaps his most withering protest came in a letter to Margaret Wilson, a convert to Catholicism, who felt she may have been received into the Church too soon. She was worried about the definition and unsettled by rumors of priests who would not give the sacraments to people who could not accept the new dogma. Newman sent her a letter on October 20 and declared: "I think there are some Bishops and Priests, who act as if they did not care whether souls were lost or not—and only wish to save souls on their own measure" (*L.D.* xxv, 216). Such an indictment of certain members of the clergy as careless and selfishly callous in the way they were exercising their pastoral responsibilities could scarcely be more damning. It touched him profoundly. Some days later, he told another friend, David Moriarty, who was the Bishop of Kerry, that such behavior "so pierces my heart, I do not know what to do—and I rise in indignation against such cruelty" (*L.D.* xxv, 223).

What he did, in fact, was develop a strategy for those who wrote to him in distress. He pleaded with them not to confuse the doctrine that had been defined with the manner in which it was passed. A letter to Catherine Froude, a longstanding friend, early in 1871 is typical of his approach. He tried to reassure her: "As little as possible was passed at the Council—nothing about the Pope which I have not myself always held—but it is impossible to deny that it was done with an imperiousness and overbearing willfulness, which has been a great scandal" (*L.D.* xxv, 262). Such remarks were a common feature of his letters at that time (*L.D.* xxv, 224, 277–278; *L.D.* xxvi, 11).

And he consoled those who were troubled further by reminding them of the lesson of history. To one he wrote:

> if you look into history, you find Popes continu-
> ally completing the acts of their predecessors, and
> Councils too—sometimes only half the truth is
> brought out at one time—I doubt not a coming
> Pope, or a coming Council, will so explain and
> guard what has now been passed by [the] late
> Council, as to clear up all that troubles us now.
> (*L.D.* xxv, 322)

And another he told: "Let us be patient, let us have faith, and a new pope, and a re-assembled Council may trim the boat" (*L.D.* xxv, 310).

These letters in particular give a sense of the fretful atmosphere at the time and how Newman handled the controversy that swirled around the defining of papal infallibility. In brief, he was against the definition for two principal reasons. First of all, he believed it to be unnecessary. Formerly definitions had been made to combat particular heresies. But that reason did not hold good in this particular instance, and, he observed, "It is dangerous to go beyond the rule of tradition in such a matter" (*L.D.* xxiv, 377). Here he was anticipating the remarks he was to make even more trenchantly to his bishop in January 1870, when he spoke of the definition as "thunder in a clear sky" and "a luxury of devotion, and not a stern painful necessity" (*L.D.* xxv, 18–19). Then connected with this first reason was the second: because the definition was unnecessary, it unsettled people's minds. He was aware of the distress that was being caused through the letters he received from those who asked for his advice. The definition made the defense of Catholicism more difficult (*L.D.* xxvi, 139).

Newman's reaction to the definition was, therefore, quite plain: while he had no difficulty in accepting it and as a Catholic at least had always held it, he was scandalized by the behavior of those who had championed it and considered the definition itself both unnecessary and pastorally disadvantageous.[4] There also remains, however, the further question of what he understood the gift of infallibility to mean.

(iii)

In 1874, when British prime minister and Catholic opponent William Gladstone lost the general election, he attributed his misfortune in part to the influence that he felt the pope had exercised in Ireland, an influence that undermined his position. He was mistaken, but that conviction led him to attack the decrees of the Vatican Council. He produced a popular pamphlet in which he claimed that on account of those decrees, Roman Catholics had forfeited their moral and mental freedom and placed their civil loyalty and duty under the pope. As citizens they were no longer to be trusted. Newman was the person to whom many people turned for an answer to these charges.

He struggled for a while before deciding how to reply, but eventually he wrote at some speed his *Letter to the Duke of Norfolk*. He struggled partly because he knew and admired Gladstone, although he believed him to be wrong in this instance; however, he also struggled because he wanted his response to offer an alternative view to the exaggerated claims that people like W.G. Ward and those who agreed with him, not to mention Archbishop Manning, were inclined to make. The situation was delicate. He asserted, however, that some Catholics could largely blame themselves for alienating Gladstone, and this was the occasion when he described the language and behavior of these enthusiasts as often irresponsible, setting the house on fire and leaving to others "the task of putting out the flame" (*Diff.* ii, 176–177).

Newman's *Letter to the Duke of Norfolk*, answering Gladstone's charges, drew material together and covered a range of particular subjects, such as the nature of the Church, the papacy, conscience, Pope Pius IX's controversial Syllabus of Errors, and issues arising from the Vatican Council itself. For our purposes, however, the core of his position emerges more precisely from his correspondence, the letters he wrote to particular individuals, responding to their concerns and anxieties and answering their questions. Reviewing those letters, four points arise regularly, points that are as essential for us today as they were in the years immediately following the First Vatican Council. In fact, when I am being questioned about infallibility, these are the issues to which almost always I find myself returning.[5]

(iv)

First of all, Newman used to insist that infallibility was an external gift. It was not some sort of inherent quality of the pope's mind, influencing every judgment he makes. In a brief, dense letter dated September 17, 1872, to one correspondent who may have been the Anglo-Catholic controversialist R.F. Littledale, he wrote: "Infallibility is not a *habit* in the Pope, or a state of mind." It was, he stressed, an external, not an internal, aid. He repeated that the pope "has no habit of infallibility in his intellect, such that his *acts cannot but* proceed from it, *must* be infallible *because* he is infallible, *imply, involve,* an infallible judgment."

It is not as though the pope cannot avoid being infallible. When, then, does he act infallibly? "He is infallible," Newman explained, *"pro re nata* [according to the circumstances], *when* he speaks *ex cathedra*—not except at particular times and on grave questions." And Newman held this view because he recognized that the pope's infallibility did not belong to him as a gift to a private person but was "that infallibility which the Church has." The pope is not infallible habitually but as the Church is infallible; he exercises his gift only when he speaks *ex cathedra* (*L.D.* xxvi, 171).

What does this expression, *ex cathedra*, mean? It roots the pope's teaching in the life of the Church. That was the second point Newman always wished to make plain. The *cathedra*, of course, is the bishop's chair, the place from which symbolically he gives his most solemn teaching.

On November 1, 1870, Newman wrote to Lady Catherine Simeon, who had become a Catholic nine years earlier and was typical of those who were distressed and confused by the new definition. He began as usual by comforting her and pointing out how limited the definition had been. Then he continued: "The whole body of theologians . . . have always held, that what the Pope said ex cathedra, was true, *when* the Bishops had received it—what has been passed, is to the effect that what he determines ex cathedra is true *independently* of the reception by the Bishops." In other words, he was pointing out what was novel in the Council's decree: when the pope acts infallibly, he does not need the consent of the bishops; he can act on his own. And then he went on, "but nothing has been passed as to *what is meant* by 'ex cathedra'—and this falls back to the Bishops and the Church to determine quite as much as before" (*L.D.* xxv, 224). Here he was recognizing that, even when acting alone, the pope's infallibility was not something merely private; it was still the infallibility of the Church, for that was what *ex cathedra* implied. Papal infallibility is never exercised in isolation. When the pope acts infallibly, he necessarily acts in relation to the Church as a whole. Already at this early stage, therefore, Newman was beginning to explore the delicate issue of the relationship between papal infallibility and the infallibility of the Church, a topic that was to become central to debates ninety years later during Vatican II.

His third point referred to the object of infallible statements and so the limits of infallibility, what it involved and what it did not. In a September 17, 1872, letter, he said it was concerned with "grave matters," which may seem rather vague, but writing to Lady Simeon he was specific: "the decree is limited to faith and morals" (*L.D.* xxv, 224). A few months later, in a letter to Catherine Froude, he declared: "certainly the Pope is not infallible beyond the Deposit of faith originally given" (*L.D.* xxv, 297). And these words, of course, anticipate the teaching of Vatican II that the infallibility with which the Church is endowed and that the pope enjoys by virtue of his office "extends as far as the deposit of divine revelation" (*Lumen Gentium*, no. 25). The first of what I referred to as Newman's preoccupations returns once more, revelation.

And we need to remember that revelation is much more than privileged information; it is the source of that essential self-knowledge the Church needs in order to be itself. Individuals who lack sufficient knowledge of themselves become mentally unbalanced, like the man who once came into my room in Oxford and declared, "I am the pope, and you are under obedience to me." Needless to say, it was not Pope John Paul II on a private visit but a man I knew well, who was schizophrenic and had stopped taking his medication. But what is sickness in individuals is still more disastrous for communities. If a community loses serious hold of its self-understanding, it may not only become unbalanced, it will lose its identity. It is what provokes schism. Revelation, the deposit of faith and morals, what we believe and how we should behave, supplies that essential self-knowledge for the Church so that it may be true to itself. And the gift of infallibility is at its service. It does not rove around, pronouncing on lesser matters. It protects and safeguards what has been revealed. The Church's infallibility, Newman told another correspondent, Alfred Plummer, on April 3, 1871, "means she can never be *permitted* to *go wrong* in the truths of revelation."

Then he indicated at once something else that those words imply, which is the fourth point on which he used to insist: "This is a negative proposition—the very idea of infallibility is a negative . . . properly speaking, inspiration is positive and infallibility is negative" (*L.D.* xxv, 309). However, this stress upon infallibility as negative should not be interpreted as diminishing it. On the contrary, it is a healthy way of recognizing that infallible definitions do not exhaust the truth they declare. What they say is not untrue, but there may still be further depths to uncover, depths that may even qualify what has presently been defined. Nevertheless, the definition is a sure guide. Only the month before writing to Plummer, he told Catherine Froude, "A Pope is not *inspired*; he has no inherent gift of divine knowledge, but when he speaks *ex cathedra*, he may say little or much, but he is simply protected from saying what is untrue" (*L.D.* xxv, 299). Even on "grave matters," as he told Littledale, "the gift [of infallibility] is negative" (*L.D.* xxvi, 171).

Infallibility, therefore, as Newman explained it, is a gift, not a habit, at the service of what has been revealed. Being a negative gift, what it declares is not exhaustive, and its exercise, whether in Council or by the pope *ex cathedra*, is always rooted in the life of the Church. That is its context.

(v)

This essential link to the Church's life was expressed by the Second Vatican Council as involving a responsibility laid on the pope and bishops, when defining dogma, to "work sedulously through the appropriate means duly to investigate . . . revelation and give it suitable expression" (*Lumen Gentium*, no. 25). Commenting on this obligation to study before defining, Bishop Christopher Butler, who was one of the council fathers, claims that failure to do so would be "a grievous sin."[6]

The part played by study in the exercise of infallibility was also something close to Newman's heart. He emphasized the need for "human means, research, consulting theologians etc." (*L.D.* xxvi, 171). He was always keen to explain the role played by the *schola theologorum*, the different theological schools. Some years before the Council, he discussed it in a letter to another acquaintance, Henry Oxenham.

After describing the way the different schools of Alexandria, Antioch, and Rome had worked on one another in the early Church, and lamenting the effective demise of all but the Roman school, he went on to describe the *schola* as not only defending, articulating, and protecting dogma, but as a teaching that is wider and fuller than apostolic dogma. It has a larger scope. He spoke of it as studying the opinion of the Church and identified it as "the arena on which questions of development and change are argued out," so that, if changes are to come, it prepares the way and prevents surprise and scandal. Without the *schola*, he observed, "the dogma of the Church would be the raw flesh without skin" (*L.D.* xxii, 99). And in his *Letter to the Duke of Norfolk*, responding to Gladstone, he stated: "None but the *Schola Theologorum* is competent to determine the force of Papal and Synodal utterances, and the exact interpretation of them is a work of time" (*Diff.* ii, 176).

The strength of these statements, of course, gave rise to another question. Isy Froude, Catherine's daughter, wrote to Newman and wondered whether "If the Schola Theologorum decides the meaning of a Pope or a Council's words, the Schola is infallible, not *they* or *he*." Newman's answer called attention to the need for words to be interpreted, however clear they might appear to be. "God is love," for example, cannot be made grounds for concluding that "*Therefore* there is no future punishment for bad men." "Some power then is needed," he told her, "to determine the general sense of authoritative words—to determine their direction, drift, limits, and comprehension, to hinder gross perversions." He described this power as "virtually the *passive infallibility* of the whole body of the Catholic people," in contrast to the "active infallibility" of the pope and bishops. The passive and the active form an alliance. "The body of the faithful never can misunderstand what the Church determines by the gift of its active infallibility." We are back to the words of St. Augustine, which had such a profound influence upon him, *Securus judicat orbis terrarum*—the universal Church is in its judgments secure of truth (*L.D.* xxvii, 337–338).

It is evident too that Newman did not regard this passive infallibility as something merely receptive, which would make it scarcely distinguishable from blind obedience. In August 1870, he wrote to another friend, Frederick Rymer, who was president of St. Edmund's College, Ware, the seminary for the Westminster Diocese. He quoted St. Augustine's words again and told him that he regarded "the general acceptance, judgment of Christendom" as "the ultimate guarantee of revealed truth" (*L.D.* xxv, 172). And in his letter to Isy Froude, he made it plain that what is infallible passively nonetheless acts. He was referring particularly to the *schola*. It acts, he affirmed, by correcting the popular misunderstandings and narrow views of teaching that may arise from active infallibility; also, because it is concerned essentially with investigating and debating issues, it keeps clear the distinction between theological truth and theological opinion. It is, Newman affirmed, "the antagonist of dogmatism." And while differences between theologians maintain liberty of thought, their unanimity "is the safeguard of the infallible decisions of the Church and the champion of faith" (*L.D.* xxvii, 337–338).

This teaching of Newman's on the role of the laity and of theologians in determining the understanding of revealed truth was a further anticipation of the view adopted by the Second Vatican Council. There it was stated:

> The universal body of the faithful who have received the anointing of the holy one, cannot be mistaken in belief. It displays this particular quality through a supernatural sense of the faith in the whole people when "from the bishops to the last of the faithful

laity," it expresses the consent of all in matters of faith and morals. (*Lumen Gentium*, no. 12)

(vi)

To express the matter briefly, therefore, the gift of infallibility according to Newman is an external, not an internal, aid, negative in character and employed only in judgments, which, while they deal with revealed truth, are nonetheless established by human means. To some this view may appear so restricted as to empty the Church's teaching on infallibility of all meaning whatsoever. But that would be a mistake. On April 3, 1871, Newman wrote to Alfred Plummer, and after pointing out that the Church teaches by human means, although assisted by grace like any other inquirer, he explained: "she has *in kind* no promise of invincible grace, which a Father or a divine, or an inquirer has not—but she has this security, that, *in order* to fulfill her office, her *out come* is always true in the matter of revelation" (*L.D.* xxv, 309). The grace is not special, but the outcome, when it concerns revelation, is assured.

This security is no mean thing. Early in 1870, while the Council was still in session, Newman in his *Grammar of Assent* discussed the distinction between infallibility and certitude. He commented on the objection that it is not possible to believe in an infallible Church without some infallible means of knowing that the Church is infallible. But the argument, he answered, rests on a confusion between infallibility and certitude. We can be certain something is true, although we sometimes make mistakes. "For example," he remarked, "I remember for certain what I did yesterday, but still my memory is not infallible." And shortly afterward he observed: "An infallible authority is certain in every particular case that may arise; but a man who is certain in some one definite case, is not on that account infallible" (*G.A.*, 224–225 [146–147]). For the Church, the particular cases will always be limited by the revealed deposit and the negative character of infallibility itself, but in those circumstances, and according to those conditions, its judgments have the assurance of a divine promise that it will not be in error.

Such a guarantee should never be underestimated. It means that the infallible Church, when teaching revealed matters, can never so mistake the message that what it teaches would lead people directly away from God. It does not prevent the Church from being in error on less essential issues, but that is only to say that the prerogative of infallibility is confined to revealed truth; nor does it mean that its teaching is always as full and as accurate as it might be, but that is only to say that the Church is human and a pilgrim and that the gift of infallibility is negative. A merely indefectible Church, on the other hand, could presumably teach something destructive of revealed truth and detrimental to salvation for many generations, and would be assured only of returning to what is true in the end. That is not enough. Unless the Church of Christ can guarantee that what it teaches on essential matters is at the very least not false, it is nothing.

Clearly such a claim is slight and not the self-aggrandizing force that those who are not Catholics sometimes fear. At the same time, such a guarantee is momentous, for it safeguards the essential purity of what the Church teaches as to be believed of necessity. This minimal claim and bedrock guarantee make up the heart of Newman's understanding of infallibility.

5

Mary, the Mother of Jesus

(i)

If the papal ministry was one obstacle on the path to Church unity, another was the controversy that arose around questions connected with Catholic teaching about Mary, the mother of Jesus. When Archbishop Michael Ramsey of Canterbury came to Rome to visit Pope Paul VI in March 1966 for their historic meeting at the Basilica of St. Paul's Outside the Walls, he stayed at the Venerable English College. I was a student there at the time. One evening he generously agreed to come upstairs to our common room to discuss any questions we students might want to raise with him. One of his remarks in particular has stuck in my memory. Asked what he regarded as the major obstacle to reunion, he answered that it was not in his view papal infallibility or the nature of authority in the Roman Church, but Mariology, or Catholic theology pertaining to Mary. And, if my memory is correct so many years later, the difficulty was not so much Mariological doctrines, the Immaculate Conception and the Assumption, as examples of the way ecclesiastical authority had been exercised, but rather the Mariological issues in themselves.

By coincidence, one hundred years earlier—in January 1866, to be exact—Newman, recently restored to respect in the eyes of his countrymen, both Anglican and Catholic, following his controversy with Charles Kingsley and the publication of his *Apologia pro Vita Sua*, addressed a public *Letter* on this very subject to Edward Pusey, his lifelong friend since their days together in Oriel (*Diff*. ii, 1–170). I want to explore the more directly ecumenical implications of their correspondence later.[1] Here it may be enough to observe that Newman had been prompted to write this *Letter* in response to a work by Pusey, *Eirenicon*[2], and in doing so, as in his *Letter to the Duke of Norfolk* some years later with regard to papal infallibility, was taking the opportunity to offer a more moderate view of Mary as an alternative to the excesses common among some Catholics, like W.G. Ward and Frederick Faber. Their extremism created an obstacle for Anglicans. He wanted others to know, "did they come to stand where I stand, what they would, and what they would not, be bound to hold concerning [the Blessed Virgin]!" (*Diff*. ii, 25). By helping others look toward Rome with more sympathy, he was addressing the very need to which Archbishop Ramsey was to draw attention in the English College a hundred years later.

(ii)

On March 25, 1832, the feast of the Annunciation, Newman preached a sermon called "The Reverence due to the Blessed Virgin Mary" (*P.S.* ii, 127–138). He was thirty-one years old, he had yet to go on the Mediterranean holiday with the Froudes, which was to have a powerful impact on him, and it was still more than a year before the Oxford Movement could be said to have begun. These were early days. Nevertheless, in this sermon he covered a remarkable range of teaching about Mary: for example, the annunciation made to her and her visit to her cousin Elizabeth; Mary as the second Eve; Mary as the mother of God's Son; Mary who as mother secures the true humanity of the child she bore; and when he referred also to her holiness and perfection, there were even those who accused him of holding the Roman Catholic doctrine of the Immaculate Conception. And there was more. All the same, in 1840, when struggling to preserve his place in the Church of England, following his crisis of the previous summer while reading about Monophysitism, he felt able to dismiss the notion that honor had been paid to Mary in the early Church. In an article he was to call his "last arrow" against Rome (*L.D.* vii, 418; *Apo.*, 134 [126]), he argued that there was no evidence of devotion to her among the apostles for there was no evidence of such devotion in the time immediately afterward. It was incredible to suppose that the apostles would not have passed their devotion on (*Ess.* ii, 15). Later, however, he changed his mind.

What made him change was his growing attention to early Church teaching. "The Fathers made me a Catholic," he told Pusey, "and I am not going to kick down the ladder by which I ascended into the Church" (*Diff.* ii, 24). And in the early Church, he discovered, Mary had often been called the second Eve. It seemed like the received teaching. He found it in the East in the writings of Justin Martyr, in the West in the writings of Tertullian, and he found it also in the writings of St. Irenaeus, who spoke for both East and West since he came from Asia Minor and was a church leader in Gaul. In Newman's view, he also represented a tradition that went back through Polycarp to the apostle John. So when he reprinted his Anglican article as a Catholic, he noted his change of view: he observed that this teaching about Mary was so widespread in the period immediately after the apostles that it must have come from them (*Ess.* ii, 15 n.). And he referred to it in his *Letter to Pusey* when he called this teaching "rudimental"; that is, "the broad outline" from which a more perfect account would develop (*Diff.* ii, 31).

The basis of the teaching arises from viewing the scene of the Fall in the Garden of Eden as a drama involving three characters: the serpent, Adam, and Eve. And when the woman and the man were sentenced for their sin, God spoke to the serpent: "I will put enmity between you and the woman, and between your offspring and hers; he will strike your head, and you will strike his heel" (Gen. 3:15). A future drama was being foretold. The scene would be reenacted:

the serpent would meet a new Adam and a second Eve; and the new Adam would be the child, the offspring, of the new Eve.

The writings of Justin (*Dialogue with Trypho*, 100), Tertullian (*De Carne Christi*, 17), and Irenaeus (*Adversus Haereses*, 3:22, 34; 5:19) are full of the parallels and contrasts between Eve and Mary (*Diff.* ii, 33–35). Newman pointed out and highlighted them: as Eve had cooperated in the fall of the human race, Mary cooperated in its salvation; as Eve had forfeited privileges by sin, Mary had earned privileges by grace; as Eve was disobedient and unbelieving, Mary was obedient and believing; as Eve was a cause of ruin to all, Mary was a cause of salvation to all; as Eve made room for Adam's fall, Mary made room for the redemption her Son won for us; and "as Eve co-operated in effecting a great evil, Mary co-operated in effecting a much greater good" (*Diff.* ii, 36). This way of arguing may be unfamiliar to us today, but it is difficult to resist the conclusion that these three authorities whom Newman used bore witness to a teaching more primitive than their own. As Newman remarked wryly, "Only suppose there were so early and broad a testimony, to the effect that our Lord was a mere man, the son of Joseph; should we be able to insist upon the faith of the Holy Trinity as necessary to salvation?" (*Diff.* ii, 38). He then illustrated this teaching from seven more sources from the fourth and fifth centuries.[3]

This tradition, then, may be solid, but it may still seem odd to lay much stress on it today. Doesn't it look more like a relic of times past than a teaching that could be significant for the present? Writing to Pusey, however, Newman moved on from it boldly to concentrate "upon two inferences, which it is obvious to draw from the rudimental teaching itself," Mary's sanctity and her dignity, or, in other words, her Immaculate Conception and her Assumption into heaven (*Diff.* ii, 44). As Eve was created in grace and her position as "the Mother of all the living" indicated her dignity, how could Mary's state of grace and dignity be any less?

(iii)

Mary's Sanctity

The doctrine of the Immaculate Conception was not new ground for Newman. In that early sermon in 1832, he asked: "What, think you, was the sanctity and grace of that human nature, of which God formed his sinless Son; knowing, as we do, 'that what is born of the flesh, is flesh'; and that 'none can bring a clean thing out of an unclean'?"[4] These were the words that had caused him to be "accused of holding the doctrine of the Immaculate Conception"; for, as he explained in 1860 to Arthur Osborne Alleyne, a Catholic convert who had returned to Anglicanism, partly on account of his difficulty with this teaching, "it was clear that I connected 'grace' with the Blessed Virgin's humanity—as if grace and nature in her case never had been separated." And he supported his view by referring to Justin, Tertullian, and Irenaeus and the way they contrasted Mary and Eve as "typical contrasts" (*L.D.* xix, 346–347). Two weeks later he wrote Alleyne an extremely long letter, which later he was to use when writing his *Letter to Pusey* (*L.D.* xix, 361–70). To Pusey he stated plainly that this teaching about the Immaculate Conception "really does seem to me bound up in the doctrine of the Fathers, that Mary is the second Eve" (*Diff.* ii, 46).

It is not surprising, then, that when Newman wrote about the Immaculate Conception, he stressed the ease of accepting such a teaching, once due attention had been made to the condition of Eve. He pointed to a common view, Anglican as well as Catholic, that Eve's state was not of nature alone, but also of grace. And this grace was not something external, a favor or outward help, but an inward gift, given to Eve from the first moment of her personal existence. And he asked, "Is it possible to deny that Mary too had this gift from the very first moment of her personal existence?" That was what he understood the doctrine of the Immaculate Conception to imply: namely, Mary's possession of the inward gift of grace, which gave her from the first that relationship with God that Eve had enjoyed at the first (*Diff.* ii, 45–46). He found it unavoidable that Mary must have been as fully endowed with grace as Eve. Had there been no fall, Newman observed, all of Eve's children "would have been conceived in grace, as in fact they were conceived in sin." So Mary, he concluded, "may be called, as it were, a daughter of Eve unfallen" (*Diff.* ii, 47).

One obvious difficulty with this approach concerns the legitimacy of contrasting the legendary Eve with the historical Mary. But even this problem may not be as intractable as it seems.

We need to remember that this contrast was never understood by Newman as something primarily historical. It was a contrast of type. Beyond a view of what might be thought actually to have happened, Eve was seen as a symbol of responsible cooperation in the fall of the human race, and Mary symbolized responsible cooperation in its restoration. So it is not so much a question of accepting Eve as symbolic as coming to terms with the symbolic character of Mary's role. And in fact as scholars have come to realize how little they know about the historical Mary, so they have become more and more aware of her power as our pattern and example.

In his final University sermon, in which Newman sketched his theory of development in religious doctrine, inspired by Luke's gospel, which speaks of Mary pondering things in her heart (Lk 2:19), he stated that Mary "symbolizes to us, not only the faith of the unlearned, but of the doctors of the Church also." She stands as a model for all, the "pattern of Faith, both in the reception and in the study of Divine Truth" (*U.S.*, 313). She is seen as the one who has accomplished what each of us hopes to achieve. To say all this is obviously not to deny a historical basis for our understanding of Mary; what actually happened supplies the ground for the symbolism; to go no further, her title as the second Eve bears eloquent testimony to her reputation for holiness in the early Church. She was, to return to Newman's phrase, "a daughter of Eve unfallen."

That expression itself, however, may give rise to a further question. Did Newman mean that Mary was untouched by the fall, that she had no need of a savior? The question depends on what is meant by original sin.

Radical Protestants have understood original sin as referring not merely to the human fall from grace and the dire consequences of that fall, but as an actual infection of human nature: original sin changed what it is to be human; thereafter we cannot avoid sinning. According to this interpretation, anyone who is unfallen must, therefore, be a different kind of human being, essentially distinct from all those others who, left to themselves, can do nothing but sin. What need could such a person have of a savior? Newman, however, demonstrated the Catholic view.

He explained that original sin does not permeate human nature, making all human acts sinful. It is instead something negative, depriving men and women of the grace that was originally given to Adam and Eve as a free gift. It enfeebles, but without contaminating. And so it is possible to be without sin in fact and therefore unfallen and, at the same time, to be a member of the fallen human race. That, according to Newman, was Mary's position.

He told Pusey:

> Protestants . . . fancy that we ascribe a different nature from ours to the Blessed Virgin, different from that of her parents, and from that of fallen Adam. We hold nothing of the kind; we consider that in Adam she died, as others; that she was included with the whole human race in Adam's sentence; that she incurred his debt, as we do. . . . (*Diff.* ii, 48)

He was making the point that Mary's freedom from original sin did not set her apart in a different kind of human nature because original sin is not essential to being human. Moreover, she enjoyed her freedom from the debt of original sin because of her savior, not in spite of him. Newman observed that "for the sake of Him who was to redeem her and us upon the Cross, to her the debt was remitted by anticipation, on her the sentence was not carried out, except indeed as regards her natural death, for she died when her time came, as others" (*Diff.* ii, 48). It was "in order to fit her to become the Mother of her and our Redeemer, to fit her mentally, spiritually for it" that she received this "special privilege" (*Diff.* ii, 49).

The very notion of privilege implies her share in our common, fallen nature. She *ought* to have been flawed as well. How else is her innocence privileged? On account of her role, Mary was preserved from original sin, while we are released from it. But the preserving and the releasing are no more than two expressions of the same redeeming work. She had need of the Savior as much as anyone.[6]

Mary's Dignity

The arguments Newman used to explain Mary's Assumption in his *Letter to Pusey* are much less likely to strike a chord today. He referred, for example, to the vision in the Apocalypse of the Woman and Child and asked whether the silence about Mary's dignity in the early Church was not evidence that it went unchallenged. He acknowledged that there were difficulties in the case he was making, but to us it may still seem too much like special pleading (see *Diff*. ii, pp. 50–61). All the same, he recognized that the image of the Woman pointed to the Church.

Then, three years later, as the First Vatican Council was beginning, the subject came up once more in a private letter to Magdalene Helbert, who was attracted to Catholicism and corresponded with Newman but was received into the Church only shortly before she died. Newman told her that, were the Assumption to be defined at the Council, "I should say that plainly it, as the Immaculate Conception, is contained in the dogma, 'Mary the Second Eve,'" and he mentioned his *Letter to Pusey*. Then he went on: "as to the Assumption, if Mary is like Eve but greater, then, as Eve would not have seen death or corruption, so, while Mary underwent death because she was a child of fallen Adam and sinned in Adam, she did not see corruption because she had more than the prerogatives of Eve" (*L.D.* xxiv, 330). Once again, the argument may not appeal to modern day as the explanation may seem too strained. But there is more to be added.

In the long letter he wrote to Alleyne in 1860, which he used when preparing his *Letter to Pusey*, Newman early on made a remark that is germane here. He was referring to the Immaculate Conception, but the point touches the doctrine of the Assumption as well.

He was explaining the difference of view taken by Catholics and Protestants in these matters. He observed:

> Catholics do not view it [the Immaculate Conception] as a substantive and independent doctrine, so much as one of a family of doctrines which are intimately united together, whereas Protestants consider it as separate from every other, and as requiring a proof of its own as fully as if it were the only thing that we knew of the Blessed Virgin. (*L.D.* xix, 362)

In other words, he was arguing that these doctrines are not to be assessed in isolation but need rather to be seen in their relationship to others and to each other. Both the Immaculate Conception and the Assumption are declarations of Mary's radical holiness in a very exact sense, a holiness, namely, that goes to the very roots of her existence.

They reveal, moreover, what our own redemption will be, when our sins have not only been forgiven but destroyed. In the words of the English Dominican Herbert McCabe, it shall be "as though sin had never been. Redemption for us will involve a rebirth from an immaculate conception." That radical holiness, which Mary's existence proclaims, is the destiny in which we hope to share: "Her Assumption is the beginning of the resurrection of all who are taken up into Christ's resurrection."[6] By drawing out inferences from her role as the second Eve, Newman himself became a witness to that belief in Mary's holiness that had been passed down, century after century. "What height of glory may we not attribute to her?" he asked in his *Letter to Pusey*, just as, more than thirty years before, he had asked in that early sermon, "Who can estimate the holiness and perfection of her, who was chosen to be the Mother of Christ?" (*Diff.* ii, 61; *P.S.* ii, 131).

(iv)

If anxiety about the doctrines of the Immaculate Conception and the Assumption is one source of Mariological controversy, another is the suspicion that praise offered to Mary distracts from the honor due to her Son. This problem surfaced in his *Letter to Pusey* when Newman examined her title as Mother of God.

When used in its approved sense, Newman explained, this phrase is neither rhetorical nor extravagant but well-weighed, grave, and dogmatic: "It intends to express that God is her Son, as truly as any one of us is the son of his own mother." This title illustrates and brings together her holiness and her greatness: "It is the issue of her sanctity; it is the origin of her greatness" (*Diff.* ii, 62). In fact, a general review of Newman's thought about Mary would show that his understanding of her is founded firmly in his perception of her dignity as the Mother of her Son.[7]

None of this, of course, was disputed by Pusey. But this teaching about Mary as the Mother of God also inspired devotion to her. And that shift from teaching about her to devotion to her was what made some people suspicious. As devotion grew, they became anxious. Pusey objected to Faber's words: "Jesus is obscured, because Mary is kept in the background."[8]

Newman, however, was not impressed by the objection. "Now I say plainly," he replied, "I never will defend or screen any one from your just rebuke, who, through false devotion to Mary, forgets Jesus. But I should like the fact to be proved first; I cannot hastily admit it." On the contrary, he argued, the evidence across Europe pointed in the other direction; "just those nations and countries have lost their faith in the divinity of Christ, who have given up devotion to His Mother, and . . . those on the other hand, who have been foremost in her honor, have retained their orthodoxy" (*Diff.* ii, 92). Devotion to Mary safeguarded faith in the divinity of Christ.

I was reminded of this argument in 1977 when I found myself reading an article by Anglican scholar Canon Donald Nicholson on "Mary: a Living Tradition in Anglicanism." He began:

On 14 August 1927 I was present at an evening
service in Wakefield Cathedral (Anglican). The
preacher was the Chamberlain of York Minster and
his theme was "Mary," the next day being the "il-
legal" feast of the Assumption. I remember his telling us that diminution in devotion to the Blessed
Virgin was invariably followed by decline in belief
in the divinity of Our Lord: unexpected and stirring words in those far-off days.[9]

And he drew to a close with words from a lecture by Bishop Eric
Kemp of Chichester: "The only reason for devotion to the Mother
is that her Son is divine, and Marian devotion is a safeguard for
the doctrine of the deity of Christ." Canon Nicholson commented:
"What had been an *outré* remark on the lips of a minor canon fifty
years ago becomes a considered judgment by a diocesan bishop
of today."[10] In the circumstances, it is difficult not to speculate on
the spur for the chamberlain's daring. Was he influenced by Newman's remark to Pusey? There may, of course, be no connection
whatever, but the coincidence is at least noteworthy.

According to Newman, therefore, the doctrines of Mary's Immaculate Conception and her Assumption bear witness to her
radical holiness, while her title as Mother of God affirms her relationship with her Son and Savior and proclaims her dignity.
Moreover, as Newman declared to Pusey, once people "recognize
the sanctity and dignity of the Blessed Virgin," it is impossible for
them not to perceive immediately that her role in heaven "is one
of perpetual intercession for the faithful" on earth (*Diff.* ii, 73).
This well of holiness in her springs up on our behalf as intercession. Nevertheless, there can be misunderstandings.

(v)

When Catholics pray to Mary, people sometimes suppose
that in this way too they are obscuring the honor due to her Son.
Shouldn't we be praying to him, not to her? But there is a difference. Our prayer to God is invocation; we call on him. Our prayer
to Mary and the saints, and indeed to one another, is intercession;

we are asking for help. The charming, rather earnest wife of an American evangelical pastor once challenged me on this very point: why did I worship Mary through prayer instead of praying to Jesus? I explained that Catholics do not really worship her but rather ask her to pray for them. The point was not immediately taken. So then I said, "When you've a problem, don't you ask your husband to pray for you?" "Of course, I do," she replied at once. Then the penny dropped.

It is natural for Christians to pray for one another. We ask each other's help. And that is what intercession means. In particular, we turn to those we admire, those who, we believe, lead good lives, people whom we judge to be holy. Holiness is the driving force of intercession (*Diff.* ii, 71). That is why we ask for Mary's help. Her holiness commends her. She is not the source of mercy; we do not invoke her, as if she were divine; but she is our advocate (*Diff.* ii, 101). We pray to her, ask for her help, trusting in her intercession. True devotion, properly understood, should cause no problems.

When it does, the cause is usually plain: devotion has become confused with doctrine. The vital distinction between them has been lost, and as a result, those with exaggerated views try to impose as essential doctrine their own favored pious practices, which at best are optional. Writing his *Letter to Pusey*, Newman also had his eye on these Catholics. The antidote was to maintain firmly the distinction between doctrine and devotion. Newman emphasized this importance (*Diff.* ii, 97; *L.D.* xxii, 90). When this distinction is secure, it restrains this devotional dogmatism and releases that authentic devotion that is the natural consequence of deep faith.

At the same time, he was also aware of something even worse, the excesses that had appalled Pusey and that he too regarded as scandalous. He attacked them without mercy. He summarized a whole range of them; for example, "that the Blessed Virgin is superior to God," "that Christ fulfilled the office of Savior by imitating her virtues," and "that His Body and Blood in the Eucharist are truly hers and appertain to her." Those views, he stated,

> seem to me like a bad dream. . . . They do but
> scare and confuse me. I should not be holier, more

> spiritual, more sure of perseverance, if I twisted my
> moral being into the reception of them; . . . I will
> have nothing to do with statements [about Mary],
> which can only be explained, by being explained
> away.

And he dismissed these excesses as "calculated to prejudice inquirers, to frighten the unlearned, to unsettle consciences, to provoke
blasphemy, and to work the loss of souls" (*Diff.* ii, 113–115).

(vi)

If deep faith in Mary, as Newman observed, soon inspired true
devotion, it seems natural to ask about his own devotion to her.
He explained his position in a private letter to Pusey in 1865.

There he confirmed his conviction that anyone entering a
church like himself should take up its practical system, "its popular catechisms and books of devotion." All the same, he insisted upon a distinction between this system and "the additions or
color which it receives in this country or that, in this class, in this
school, or that" (*L.D.* xxii, 100). These remarks merely echoed
the position he ascribed to himself in his *Apologia*. Certain extravagant continental devotions in Mary's honor had been, he
confessed, his "great *crux* as regards Catholicism." He went on:
"I say frankly, I do not fully enter into them now; I trust I do
not love her the less, because I cannot enter into them. They
may be fully explained and defended; but sentiment and taste
do not run with logic: they are suitable for Italy, but they are not
suitable for England" (*Apo.*, 195 [176–177]). His own spiritual
temperament, he added, shaped his disposition, that intense
awareness of the divine presence—of himself and his Creator as
the two absolute and luminously self-evident beings—made any
extravagance unthinkable (*Apo.*, 195, 4 [177, 18]).

He made his position plain in the *Letter* he published: "May
God's mercy keep me from the shadow of a thought, dimming the
purity or blunting the keenness of that love of Him, which is our
sole happiness and our sole salvation!" What then of Mary? She is

> only our Mother by divine appointment, given
> us from the Cross; her presence is above, not on
> earth; her office is external, not within us . . . her
> power is indirect. It is her prayers that avail, and
> her prayers are effectual by the *fiat* of Him who is
> our all in all. (*Diff.* ii, 83–84)

If those words seem restrained, they should not be mistaken for a lack of true devotion.[11] True devotion is warm, generous, and free; it defies criticism (*Diff.* ii, 80). However, it must never become a slave of extravagance. For Newman it never did.

It seems to me that Newman's appeal to the Church fathers, his awareness of the distinction between doctrine and devotion, while recognizing their relationship, his attention to Mary's holiness and dignity, and his hostility to excess are all points of ecumenical significance. Let me return to Archbishop Ramsey.

(vii)

A week after his meeting with Pope Paul VI in 1966, Dr. Ramsey visited Newman's Oxford college, Oriel, to open a symposium in Newman's honor. He suggested that renewal for both Anglicans and Catholics would come from recapturing something of Newman's spirit, which he characterized as the spirit of scriptural holiness. That holiness is the basis of Christian unity.[12] Moreover, its outstanding model, we may add, is the mother of Jesus.

In an early Catholic letter, Newman acknowledged his debt to Mary: "I have ever been under her shadow, if I may say it. My College was St. Mary's, and my Church; and when I went to Littlemore, there, by my previous disposition, our Blessed Lady was waiting for me" (*L.D.* xii, 153–154). And so it was. Oriel is formally St. Mary's College; the University Church where Newman was vicar is the church of St. Mary the Virgin; and his church at Littlemore is dedicated to St. Mary the Virgin and St. Nicholas. Shortly after writing this letter, he named his oratory church in Birmingham after her Immaculate Conception. He remained under her shadow to the end.

6

Serving the Laity

(i)

When the Second Vatican Council began on October 11, 1962, there were those who did not expect it to last very long, perhaps no more than a single session. They realized that the documents that had been prepared for the assembled bishops would no doubt be amended, but they were quite confident that they would also be approved. The Council would be over very soon. That expectation, however, was not fulfilled. Many bishops were critical of the documents, their content and their character. And beyond that there was something else. It took almost the full eight weeks of that first session to articulate it: what had been prepared was too diffuse. It needed focus. On December 2, 1962, the Archbishop of Milan, Cardinal Giovanni Battista Montini, who barely six months later would become Pope Paul VI, wrote to his diocesan newspaper, *L'Italia*, and described this session as a running-in period. Nevertheless, it had served its purpose. These weeks, he concluded,

had helped the Council identify its central theme: "the Church."[1]
Three days later he made the same point in the Council chamber.

As the council fathers explored that theme more closely, they
came to concentrate less on an approach that understood the
Church principally in terms of what distinguished its members
from each other—in other words, its hierarchical structure—and
gave priority instead to what united them, their common baptism.
This was the source from which the revival of the understanding
of the Church as *koinωnia* (*koinonia* or communion) sprang. Emphasis was placed on the unity of all the faithful, and it meant,
therefore, that the lay faithful came into their own. There is a
rather clumsy sentence in the eventual Decree on the Lay Apostolate: "Within christian communities [the laity's] activity is so
necessary that without it the pastors' apostolate cannot generally
(*plerumque*) attain its full effect" (*Apostolicam Actuositatem*, no. 10).
It may be read in a highly clerical way, as though the poor laity are
simply topping up what the clergy have not managed to achieve
on their own; in fact, however, it is pointing to the essential need
for activity in the Church to be properly integrated.

As this awareness of the lay apostolate emerged, there were
those who saw Newman as one of its pioneers. They pointed in
particular to an article he had written for the *Rambler* in 1859,
"On Consulting the Faithful in Matters of Doctrine." It had caused
him trouble then; now it was being recognized as prophetic.[2] We
must consider it. But it would be a mistake to see that one article
as somehow an isolated instance in Newman's life and work. His
commitment to the laity and the service he gave them were profound and lifelong.

(ii)

Newman's Oxford, of course, was predominantly clerical. The
university he knew both as an undergraduate and as a don was
largely in the charge of unmarried clergymen. Only the heads of
the colleges could be married. When a young don, who would
usually have been ordained, decided to marry, he had to resign

his fellowship and seek a parish living. There were many in the gift of the colleges.

As we have noticed already, however, even at an early age, Newman's pastoral instinct made him sensitive to the influence of those among whom he found himself. [3] He went to his first curacy at St. Clement's as an earnest evangelical Anglican, but his stern viewpoint was softened by the sheer goodness of the people he met there. It was not possible for him to believe that most of them would be damned. He was attentive to his parishioners as they really were. Then, as a tutor at Oriel, he saw his duty as extending beyond intellectual instruction; there was a moral dimension as well. Those who were hostile viewed this approach as theological indoctrination, but others compared it to the attention given to pupils by only the very best private tutors. [4] Afterward, when the Oxford Movement was at its height while he was vicar of St. Mary the Virgin, the University Church, he delivered his *Lectures on the Prophetical Office* and afterward his *Lectures on Justification*. These were not formal university lectures but were given in the Adam de Brome Chapel in St. Mary's to deepen the understanding of those who attended them. And then again the scope and style of his *Parochial Sermons* should not be forgotten. Moreover, while vicar of St. Mary's, he had the parish church built at Littlemore, the place that was to become so important to him, as he struggled to determine his future between Canterbury and Rome and where he wrote his *Essay on Development*. On my first visit there in 1966, I was shown around by a woman whose grandfather as a young boy had heard Newman preach his last Anglican sermon there in 1843. He had moved those who heard him by speaking about "The Parting of Friends" (*S.D.*, 395–409). All these activities, integral to his Anglican life, point to his commitment to serving lay people. They also bear witness to his later assertion—one of those recurring themes or preoccupations that shaped his life— that education had always been his line (*A.W.*, 259).

Then, besides these features of his Anglican life, the vocation he chose as a Catholic priest also had a bearing on his approach to the laity. When he was sent to Rome to prepare for ordination, he was unsure what kind of priest he should be. He wondered about becoming a Jesuit or a Dominican, a Vincentian or a Redemptorist, but he found himself drawn in fact by the person of St. Philip Neri.

Philip was born in Florence in 1515, but he came to Rome as a young man. He lived simply and helped people generously. They were attracted by the warmth and gentleness of his personality. His ministry became so effective that he was recognized as the apostle of Rome for his own time. Some of those who were influenced by him gathered to join him in prayer in the small oratory in the Church of San Girolamo della Carità. These, of course, were largely lay people. When these meetings began, Philip was still a layman himself. When he was ordained eventually in 1551, he and those who had gathered with him who were also priests became known as Oratorians. Although they lived in community, they were secular priests. They took no vows and were able to keep their own possessions. Philip was not interested in eye-catching display. His ideal was "to love to be unknown" (O.S., 241). This was the model of priestly life and ministry that caught Newman's heart and imagination. In many ways it reflected and re-created for him as a Catholic priest the life in community with unmarried clergymen that he had cherished as a fellow of Oriel. And the Oratorian parish in Birmingham also meant that he continued the ministry he had exercised in Oxford and at Littlemore.

The bond that bound Oratorians together was one of love and a sense of family, rather than the rule of authority and obedience. That aspect also was in tune with Newman's capacity for friendship.

There is a kind of paradox here. Newman was sometimes described as a man who was never less alone than when alone; there was something reserved and solitary about him. All the same, he had an extraordinary gift for friendship. His many letters bear witness to that, and those, for example, to the women who were his friends illustrate the fact beyond dispute.[5] Then in his poem "A Thanksgiving," written in October 1829, he spoke of "Blessings of friends, which to my door/ Unask'd, unhoped, have come"

(*V.V.*, 46). Newman saw in friendship love made real. He was not persuaded that it is better to love everyone in general. When he preached about the beloved disciple two years later, he saw in the friendship between Jesus and John an example to follow. He stated his conviction that "the best preparation for loving the world at large, and loving it duly and wisely, is to cultivate an intimate friendship and affection towards those who are immediately about us" (*P.S.* ii, 52–53).

Here, too, I gladly and gratefully acknowledge Newman's influence on me. These words struck a chord when I first read them many years ago. And now, looking back, I wonder how I could have survived my long years of celibate priesthood without my friends. There are, of course, those nowadays who can make no sense of such relationships, uncluttered by physical sexual activity. They doubt whether they actually exist. But they do. Just as the best marriages are often built as much on friendship as on passion, so many of us who are single, whether by choice or chance or commitment to celibacy, know what it means to delight in our friends. I have paid tribute to mine elsewhere and am happy to do so again. They offer me "a promise of merriment, good talk, wise advice, and generous hospitality. . . . I hold them in love and believe I am loved by them. They do not diminish the ministry I offer. They are pure gift for which I give constant thanks."[6] As well as my own experience, Newman's conviction also underlies these words. We cannot love in general unless we love in particular.

And while he loved his friends, he valued marriage too. On January 12, 1854, preaching at the religious profession as a Visitation nun of Mary Anne Bowden, the daughter of John Bowden, who had died in 1844 but who had been his friend since they were undergraduates together at Trinity College, Oxford, he spoke powerfully of her religious calling, but not before he had spoken also of marriage as the "one central and supreme attachment to which none other can be compared." These words are full of power. Children leave parents, he went on, as Jesus left Mary, but marriage is indestructible and recalls "the everlasting ineffable love with which the Father loves the Son who is in His bosom and the

Son the Father who has from all eternity begotten Him."[7] If these words seem fanciful and unrealistic in a society scarred by marital breakdown, we ought still to be able to recognize the ideal.

His pastoral ministry as an Anglican, his Oratorian vocation, and his valuing of friendship and marriage as paths to fulfilling the great commandment of love all point to the context within which his service of lay people was realized. That service was plain in his Catholic years, in particular during his time as rector of the university he established in Dublin and then afterward during the brief but turbulent period when he was editor of the *Rambler*. In themselves these two episodes are distinct, but they can also be connected.

(iii)

On January 21, 1863, there is an entry in Newman's journal that still makes for somber reading. He was chronicling his life since he had become a Catholic in 1845, and he was perhaps at his lowest point. The mood was dark, even depressive. He acknowledged how little he personally seemed to have done as a Catholic. It was said, for example, that Manning and Faber made converts, but he did not. However, he was reluctant, as he put it, "to make hasty converts of educated men, lest they should not have counted the cost, and should have difficulties after they have entered the Church" (*A.W.*, 257–258). And he went on to lament the condition of Catholics in England, who "from their very blindness, cannot see that they are blind." Newman's wish was to help them assess the arguments they took for granted and examine their position with regard to the culture of the day; then, as their views developed, they would intellectually become more mature. In other words, he wanted to educate them. This was the particular place where he declared that education, that fourth major preoccupation or theme, was his "line": "Now from first to last, education, in this large sense of the word, has been my line" (*A.W.*, 259).

This concern for education was evident most dramatically in his work to found the Catholic University in Dublin. He had been invited to go there in 1851. Earlier that very year, quite independently, he had articulated his ideal:

> I want a laity, not arrogant, not rash in speech, not disputatious, but men who know their religion, who enter into it, who know just where they stand, who know what they hold, and what they do not, who know their creed so well, that they can give an account of it, who know so much of history that they can defend it.

These words resonate deeply with me. I forced myself to write the text of my book *The Catholic Faith*, which was published in 1986 while I was a chaplain at Oxford, by preparing the chapters first as lectures. The lecture series was called "An Account of Catholicism." And I spoke and wrote for the same purpose as Newman. I can make his words my own: "I want an intelligent, well-instructed laity" (*Prepos.*, 390). I was aware of questions raised by students, whether Catholic or not, by an older generation, curious about or bewildered by the Second Vatican Council, and a still older generation who had never been prepared for change at all. Each in their different ways had urgent needs. It was Newman's preoccupation, but in my own setting.

The invitation to go to Dublin had come to Newman from Archbishop Paul Cullen of Armagh, who soon afterward was transferred to Dublin and later made a cardinal. Newman gave himself to the project with great generosity for seven years.

The plan itself had been proposed by the Irish bishops as an alternative to the Queen's Colleges, which Robert Peel had established in Ireland. These colleges were unacceptable to the bishops because they excluded all religious teaching and they were open to the members of any church and to nonbelievers alike. Oxford and Cambridge, on the other hand, still imposed religious tests at that time, which made them at least in principle unavailable to Catholics. Here, then, was an opportunity to create a Catholic university for Catholics from the entire English-speaking world. Newman hoped students would come from America as well as England. He had in mind a kind of Oxford ideal transposed to the banks of the Liffey. "Curious it will be," as he observed to his friend Catherine Froude, "if Oxford is imported into Ireland" (*L.D.* xiv, 389). He was also keen on having lay professors, and in the event twenty-seven of the thirty-two he appointed were laymen.

However, it proved to be a heartbreaking exercise. The Irish bishops had something much less ambitious in view, more of a Catholic training college than a university. And they disagreed among themselves. At the same time, Newman found Cullen more and more difficult to work with. As demands were also increasing in Birmingham, he resigned finally in 1858 and returned to his oratory.

A considerable literature has grown up around this initiative. At the heart of it is what many people have regarded as a masterpiece, Newman's discourses on university education, which he published as *The Idea of a University*. His biographies examine it; there have been specialist studies, discussions, and controversies about it; and in 1976 Ian Ker produced his masterly critical edition. It is not necessary or practicable to examine those matters again here. But there are some points worth considering that have a more immediate bearing on Newman's service of the laity.

It is natural to ask, for example, whether his *Idea of a University* still has something to offer us today. It was the question examined by John Roberts in 1990, the centenary of Newman's death. He revisited Newman's discourses and was ideally equipped to do so.[8] A leading British historian, Roberts, who died in 2003, had also been vice chancellor of Southampton University and then, from 1984 to 1994, he was warden of Merton College, Oxford. He was in the thick of the educational debate in recent times.

So does Newman's *Idea* still have something to offer the modern world? Roberts was not easily persuaded. While he acknowledged the subtlety of Newman's style and carefully qualified arguments, which are often more nuanced than they may seem at first, he felt that our circumstances today are too different, "utterly remote from the academic world taken for granted by Newman" (*Newman After a Hundred Years*, 198). Who could disagree? We may, for instance, still like to see knowledge as an end in itself, but so much of what goes on in universities now "is consciously a means to useful ends," training for a career (*Newman After a Hundred Years*, 201). Newman was far removed from that attitude and from "the realities of modern universities urged by society to give greater attention to the social utility of their 'outputs'" (*Newman After a Hundred Years*, 202–203). Then again, Newman held that universities should in principle teach all branches of knowledge (*Idea*, 440), yet what he was wanting, Roberts observed, is in practice "impossible" (*Newman After a Hundred Years*, 204–205). And in any case, our fragmented, postmodern society is very different from the integrated vision of society with its unchanging values in which Newman believed. And there is more. We don't need to review it all here. In brief, Roberts was saying, universities nowadays have developed in ways very different from the one Newman envisaged.

So has Newman, therefore, nothing to offer us? But that would not be true either. There is something. Roberts described it as "a vision with which those of us who are concerned with education should from time to time try to refresh ourselves." He noted that, while we should not strive to force Newman's *Idea* to fit our needs, we could still be inspired and stimulated by it. His vision can encourage us "to defend values now under threat." And Roberts went on:

> It is helpful to recall that an educated man is not a man who knows certain things, but a man whose mind has been formed in a certain way and who can take up a certain stance when confronted with a new experience. (*Newman After a Hundred Years*, 221–222)

Newman and his contemporaries were often formidably learned; they knew a very great deal. In today's terms, they were strong on content; but beyond content, they excelled at competence.

So if Newman's vision is to be respected, it is also important to recognize it for what it is, to be aware of its limitations, as he was.

Liberal education produces the gentleman. In the *Idea*, Newman offered a description of such a person, a description that has become
well-known. There is much to be admired: "a cultivated intellect,
a delicate taste, a candid, equitable, dispassionate mind, a noble
and courteous bearing in the conduct of life." These qualities were
the fruit of the liberal education Newman was championing. All
the same, he declared, "they are no guarantee for sanctity or even
for conscientiousness" (*Idea*, 120–121 [110]). That was his concern.
Greater knowledge, deeper learning, admirable in themselves, cannot ensure moral improvement. And he reinforced his point with
an unforgettable image: "Quarry the granite rock with razors, or
moor the vessel with a thread of silk; then may you hope with such
keen and delicate instruments as human knowledge and human
reason to contend against those giants, the passion and the pride
of man" (*Idea*, 121 [111]). Newman needed something more for his
Catholic university.

What he wanted, in his desire for an education that would be
at the service of the laity, was a relationship between intellectual
excellence and religious commitment for which they were both
truly as one, united, while they still maintained their distinct in-
tegrities. He set out this viewpoint in the first of a series of sermons he preached in Dublin in 1856 and 1857.

He dismissed out of hand the charge that by advocating this
union between intellect and religion he was countenancing cen-
sorship, "ecclesiastical supervision" of intellectual matters. Nor
was he interested in compromise, as though each partner had to
yield something. "I wish the intellect to range with the utmost
freedom, and religion to enjoy an equal freedom," he declared.
His driving concern was personal. He wanted what was intellectual and what was religious to be properly integrated within the
same individual. "It will not satisfy me, what satisfies so many,"
he explained, "to have two independent systems, intellectual and
religious, going at once side by side, by a sort of division of labor,
and only accidentally brought together." He was utterly opposed
to any such division. And he summed up his ideal: "I want the

intellectual layman to be religious, and the devout ecclesiastic to be intellectual" (*O.S.*, 13).

In a later sermon in the same series, Newman took up this theme again. He did so by dividing saints into two categories. There are those, he said, who are "so absorbed in the divine life" that they seem altogether disconnected from human life and its affairs, and then there are others "in whom the supernatural combines with nature, instead of superseding it." In them, grace invigorates, elevates, and ennobles nature. They are "not the less men, because they are saints." And he continued:

> The world is to them a book, to which they are drawn for its own sake, which they read fluently, which interests them naturally,—though, by the reason of the grace which dwells within them, they study it and hold converse with it for the glory of God and the salvation of souls. (*O.S.*, 91–93)

Newman certainly admired the first group, but he was inspired by the second.

This is the vision that has also inspired me. It looks to Jesus of Nazareth as the one who was as truly divine as he was truly human, as truly human as he was truly divine. And so, as a university chaplain, I urge members of the university that our share in Christ's life must not be at the expense of our humanity:

> Our spirituality and our living witness must engage with our world, our surroundings, our conditions. In that sense, it is not enough to be in the world, but not of it; we have to be both in the world *and of the world*. As aliens, we can never reclaim it. We have to be at home here if we are to bear witness effectively.[9]

And as a seminary rector, I have insisted on the need to discover the identity of those who are ordained through recognizing their place within the community, not by simply setting them apart.[10] I again acknowledge Newman's influence.

In Dublin, therefore, although he spoke of "the idea" of a university, Newman was not simply laying out a master plan, a Platonic ideal of university education at large, but more particularly he was responding to the demands of his own circumstances there and encouraging a vision in which intellectual training, moral discipline, and religious commitment were combined. It was not a vision he found easy to make real. He was constantly frustrated, and eventually he resigned as rector on November 12, 1858.

(iv)

Once he was settled back in Birmingham, however, he was soon disturbed again. He was drawn into the crisis surrounding the *Rambler*, which many people regarded as the finest Catholic periodical of its kind in the English-speaking world. But the bishops were becoming increasingly impatient with its more liberal tone. They were especially irritated by its editor, Richard Simpson, who was a good man and a devoted Catholic, but someone also unafraid of criticizing them. The bishops were not amused. Some of them wanted to censure the paper in their pastoral letters. To avoid that and the scandal it might cause, Newman's bishop, Ullathorne, asked Newman, first of all, to persuade Simpson to resign. And Newman, who was friendly with Simpson, was able to do so. But then the question arose about a successor. Who was to be editor in Simpson's place? It had to be someone acceptable both to the *Rambler*'s proprietors and to the bishops. It quickly became clear that Newman was the obvious choice. And his very commitment to serving the laity, to their education in the broad and deep sense, which had also guided his work in Dublin, led him to accept.

Newman too, like Ullathorne, had been critical at times of Simpson's tone. Nevertheless, he liked him and shared his principles. In the first issue for which he was responsible, therefore, in May 1859, Newman wrote positively about the importance of consulting the laity in something that concerned them closely. The issue was the controversy at that time about the lack of Catholic representation on the Royal Commission on Elementary

Education. The Catholic Poor Schools Committee had probably been at fault, but Simpson had seemed critical of the way the bishops had handled the matter. That was a significant feature of the crisis that had prompted his removal. Newman in his first issue dealt with the bishops generously; he made it plain that no disrespect toward them had been intended. But he was not prepared to let the matter pass without comment. He observed: "If even in the preparation of a dogmatic definition the faithful are consulted, as lately in the instance of the Immaculate Conception [in 1854], it is at least as natural to anticipate such an act of kind feeling and sympathy in great practical questions," such as education (*L.D.* xix, 129, n.3). He apologized if the words used before or their tone seemed disrespectful, but went on to argue that there was no disrespect in assuming that the bishops would want to know the views of the laity on so great a question.

He was wrong. And his carefully chosen words provoked Dr. John Gillow, a priest on the staff of the seminary at Ushaw College, near Durham, to protest. Gillow regarded the notion that the laity might be consulted in matters of doctrine as virtually heresy. He and Newman exchanged courteous letters, and the point at issue between them was settled, although it flared again later. But opposition to the *Rambler* in certain quarters was relentless.

Ullathorne himself had become uncomfortable with the direction affairs were taking and called on Newman at the oratory to discuss the situation. This was the well-known occasion when, according to Newman's memorandum of their meeting, Ullathorne at one point asked him, "Who are the laity?" And Newman answered "that the Church would look foolish without them—*not* those words" (*L.D.* xix, 141). During the conversation, he also remarked to Ullathorne that it would in fact be a relief to give up the *Rambler*, and to his surprise, Ullathorne encouraged him to do so. It was not a command, more a suggestion, but one that Ullathorne made eagerly. And so Newman decided he would resign. He could not do so immediately, of course. He had to take responsibility for one more issue, due for July, and he decided to use the opportunity to explore further the issue Gillow had challenged. That was his reason for writing his article "On Consulting the Faithful in Matters of Doctrine." It is packed with examples about the bishops in the fourth century who had largely caved in to the heresy known as Arianism, while the lay faithful resisted it. In this outstanding instance, their fidelity had safeguarded the faith of the Church.

The immediate consequences for Newman personally were painful. Those who opposed him complained to Rome. He was accused of undermining the teaching authority of the bishops. Rome asked for an explanation, and he offered one, but his offer was not passed on. Silence, therefore, ensued. While he thought all was well, Rome thought he had refused its request. Little by little, Newman became aware that something was amiss. In the midst of the gloom, during that dark period in his life, he composed a memorandum about the *Rambler* affair on November 28, 1862. One sentence reads: "All would have been well, but for the unlucky paragraph in my July Number on the Arianizing Hierarchy" (*L.D.* xix, 151). The matter was not resolved until 1867, when his friend and fellow Oratorian Ambrose St. John visited Rome. The incident was typical of Newman's fortunes at that time. We do not need to discuss it further. It has been examined thoroughly elsewhere.[11] All the same, we should notice the core of Newman's position, what he understood consulting the laity to mean. It may guide us still. He identified five points in particular.[12]

What roused Gillow was Newman's specific reference to consulting the laity in preparing a dogmatic definition. In the panegyric at his funeral, Gillow's lectures and replies to questions were described as having "all the precision and cogency of a mathematical problem."[13] To someone with such a way of thinking, Newman's words, as he told him in a letter, implied that "the infallible portion [of the Church] would consult the fallible with a view to guiding itself to an infallible decision" (*L.D.* xix, 134, n. 3). But Newman in his answer insisted that this view misread his meaning. He was speaking of consulting as it is used in English every day, not principally as asking an opinion but rather to discover a fact. That was the first point he identified. He offered the example of "consulting a barometer about the weather. The barometer does not give us its opinion, but ascertains for us a fact." And he held his ground, refusing to concede to Gillow that infallibility lies exclusively in the teaching Church. He drew on the authority of the Jesuit theologian Giovanni Perrone, whom he had known in Rome in 1847, to argue that infallibility resides in both those who teach and those who are taught; they are as one, "as a figure is contained both on the seal and on the wax" (*L.D.* xix, 135–136). The laity, according to Newman, ought to be consulted as witnesses so that their mind may be known. He made the same point again years later during the First Vatican Council (*L.D.* xxv, 172).

The second point Newman identified was what he called "a sort of instinct, or φρονημα, deep in the bosom of the mystical body of Christ." This instinct may be hard to define but is not so difficult to recognize. It corresponds with what he referred to as the illative sense in his *Grammar of Assent*.[14] Years earlier, in one of his university sermons, he had referred to it implicitly when he noted how in practical matters, "when their minds are really roused, men commonly are not bad reasoners" (*U.S.*, 211). We have an instinct for the right way to proceed. Whether we are "gifted or not," we have an inward faculty. It inspired another of his unforgettable images. He likened this inward faculty to skillful mountaineering, making progress like "a clamberer on a steep cliff, who, by quick eye, prompt hand, and firm foot, ascends how he knows not himself, by personal endowments and by practice, rather than by rule, leaving no track behind him, and unable to teach another" (*U.S.*, 257). Newman had confidence in human reason.

All the same, there is an obvious question. Such an instinct may be identified in individuals, but can it be found in communities? Many would be skeptical, but I am not. Think of the communities you know, the groups to which you belong. For years while living in Oxford, I would see visitors on guided tours being shown around the university. They would be taken into many colleges and admire them. But by the evening I suspect it had all become a bit of a blur. They could not remember how to distinguish between

Exeter, Lincoln, and Jesus, or Trinity and St. John's, or Corpus and
Oriel. They all seemed the same. But to the members of those colleges, their distinctiveness was evident. Each community had its
own character, its own identity, and its own self-understanding.
And so the Church. The larger the community, the more complex the exercise, investigating and exploring, but the reality is the
same. There is a mind that can be determined.

And the witness of the laity that consultation determines and
the instinctive, inward faculty that articulates that witness emerges
Newman explained, in part under the direction of the Holy Spirit
and partly as an answer to prayer. These are the third and fourth
points he identified. The authentic life of the community derives
from the Spirit dwelling within believers, who are sensitive to and
respond to what they have received. This is not cheap grace but
the fruit of costly commitment. Then what they perceive becomes
known in their prayer, not as the canonizing of casual whims, but
the result of painstaking discernment.

Such authentic life in the community displays one further
characteristic, the fifth point in the process Newman outlined. He
called it "jealousy of error." Put simply, we may say that, where
life is authentic, it realizes very soon when something has gone
wrong. We see it sometimes physically in surgery, to use an example that could never have occurred to Newman during his time:
when an organ has been transplanted, heart or kidney, there is the
danger of rejection. And in general, when opinions or decisions
are proposed to it as its own, a community will recognize almost
at once when they are not. The discord will be evident.

That in brief was what Newman meant by consulting the laity.
It was a process designed to determine what the community believed in fact, based on the confidence that it knew its own mind.
That confidence was all the more secure because the lay faithful
lived a life rooted in the Spirit, to whom they were responsive in
prayer. And such a spiritual life was impatient of error; it would
recognize very soon what did not ring true.

Newman then went on to illustrate the part played by lay witness in the history of the Church, and at the end of his article, he

concluded, "each constituent portion of the Church has its proper functions, and no portion can be safely neglected . . . there is something in the 'pastorum et fidelium *conspiratio*,' which is not in the pastors alone." [15] He was emphasizing the value of what was done in common, and he argued that the clergy should seek to encourage the lay faithful; otherwise, he observed, if they cut them off from the study of doctrine and from contemplation, and required from them only "a *fides implicita*," then that unthinking acceptance "in the educated classes will terminate in indifference, and in the poorer in superstition."[16] People need to be involved, to contribute, to recognize the part they have to play.

It was the natural conclusion from what he had just illustrated, but it was a startling conclusion for those days, when the laity were regarded as "boys eternal,"[17] and the accepted atmosphere breathed of clericalism and condescension. We, however, can see in it a modest anticipation of that emphasis on the unity of all the baptized that was to gain recognition at Vatican II.

(v)

Newman's entire life, both Anglican and Catholic, was devoted to the service of the lay faithful. And during his Catholic life, he tried to serve the laity in many ways besides his work in Dublin and his editing of the *Rambler*. He founded, for example, the Oratory School, which was a great labor and also caused him much heartache at times; and his attempt also to establish an oratory in Oxford was driven by the same concern, to be of service to Catholics there. However, I have concentrated here on these two episodes in particular, his work for the Catholic University in Dublin, where he tried to establish a way of offering the lay faithful a deeper, fuller education, and his experience as editor of the *Rambler*, where he championed and tried to defend their role. Both episodes caused him great sorrow. Neither can be regarded as a clear success at the time. But let me leave the final word to Newman scholar John Coulson:

Newman's abiding vision was that, in the dark
days that were approaching and have now inevitably come upon us, the fullness of the Catholic idea
demanded that the intellectual layman become religious and the devout ecclesiastic intellectual. He
had hoped that it was his vocation to bring about
the means by which this might be achieved—by
his University, his school, his house at Oxford, and
his support for the work of *The Rambler*. But it was
not to be so. His was that greater vocation still: to
witness, by the way in which he met and mastered
the indifference, hostility, persecution, and tardy
recognition of his Catholic life to the very embodi-
ment of that ideal he had devoted his life to foster:
the practice of the saintly intellect.[18]

7

Seeking Church Unity

(i)

In the library of the Venerable English College, Rome, there is a scrapbook filled with articles cut out of newspapers that feature former members of the college. Many have become bishops or held other responsible positions in the Church. As a student there in the 1960s, I used to enjoy browsing through it. The earlier pieces, going back decades, frequently told stories of clashes between these former students and their Anglican or Free Church counterparts. The tone was combative, often abrasive. But then there was a change. Soon after the election of Pope John XXIII in October 1958, the mood became quite different. There was a move away from conflict in favor of greater understanding; controversy gave way to dialogue; and dialogue became discussion and conversation, so that friendships began to be formed. The shift was unmistakable. The desire for Christian unity was gathering momentum.

It may seem natural to assume that Newman would have little to offer in these matters. That someone who was for long an influence in the Church of England should, upon changing his allegiance, so to speak, be regarded as influential still, seems improbable at best. Yet that assumption is mistaken. Soon after that change, his loyal friend Edward Pusey spoke of his conversion as "perhaps the greatest event which has happened since the Communion of the Churches has been interrupted."[1] And he gave his reason: "If anything could open their eyes to what is good in us, or soften in us any wrong prejudices against them, it would be the presence of such a one, nurtured and grown to ripeness in our Church, and now removed to theirs."[2] That may seem too optimistic. Nevertheless, the Oxford Newman Symposium in 1966 declared: ". . . if we wish to find common elements which, when studied from the differing Christian standpoints, set the agenda for our mutual growth towards unity, then we need go no farther back in history than to Newman."[3]

Those hostile to Newman will, of course, disagree; they find him to be a barrier instead; but those more sympathetic will regard him as a bridge. What commended him in particular were his credentials, the qualities he brought to ecumenical debate. Stephen Dessain identified four of them: the way he acknowledged what was true and valuable among Christians in spite of separation, his realism about the causes of division, his recognition of where Catholicism fell short, and his desire to offer a complete and balanced account of Christian truth.[4] These were major attributes, but still the path was rocky.

(ii)

One constant personal irritant for Newman as a Catholic were the rumors that would circulate with tedious regularity about his disillusionment with the Church he had joined and his imminent return to Anglicanism. In June 1862, during that gloomy period of his life after his time in Dublin and his involvement with the *Rambler*, and before Kingsley's attack provoked his *Apologia*, one newspaper, the *Globe*, reported the rumor again with great assurance. In a blistering response, Newman spoke of his unwavering trust in the Catholic Church, his "unclouded faith in her creed," and his "supreme satisfaction in her worship, discipline, and teaching." He denied outright that he would ever leave and went on to describe Protestantism as "the dreariest of possible religions." The thought of the Anglican service, he stated, made him shiver, and the thought of the Thirty-Nine Articles made him shudder. He would be a fool, he said, to return to the Church of England (*L.D.* xx, 215–216).

These words, of course, pained his estranged Anglican friends, but as Newman explained to one of them, Charles Crawley, they referred to Protestantism and the Anglican system, not to people, and they were used to force Protestants "to put out of their minds the hope of my ever coming back to them." They were "the deliberately chosen and studied means" of bringing the tiresome rumors to an end (*L.D.* xx, 234–236). Newman's personal feelings were very different and became evident two years later when he wrote his *Apologia*: ". . . the Church of England has been the instrument of Providence in conferring great benefits on me" (*Apo.*, 341 [297]). Old friends realized how deeply he cared for them still. Here was that first credential, the acknowledging of what is true and valuable among others.

And it had always been so. Even in his early Catholic years, he had recoiled from attacks on the Church of England (*L.D.* xiv, 207). He valued what he had received from it. In 1860, for example, he explained to Edgar Estcourt, a former Anglican clergyman who was now Bishop Ullathorne's secretary and treasurer of the Birmingham Diocese, his reasons for opposing the building of a Catholic church in Oxford. He regarded the plan as unnecessarily controversial and likely to weaken the Church of England, when Anglican Oxford was in practice at that time, he pointed out, "a breakwater against Unitarianism, fanaticism, and infidelity." And he declared his own debt: "Catholics did not make us Catholics; Oxford made us Catholics. At present Oxford surely does more good than harm" (*L.D.* xix, 352). These words are the more striking because of the way they contrast with some of Manning's. Newman's attempt in his *Letter to Pusey* to offer, as we have seen,[5] a more moderate account of teaching about the Blessed Virgin

than Faber and Ward's had not pleased him. He regarded Newman's work as "worldly," a diluting of Catholic doctrine. And he
declared: "It is the old Anglican, patristic, literary, Oxford tone
transplanted into the Church."[6] While Newman seemed to value
his past and respectfully and affectionately carry it with him into
his future, so far as he could, Manning seemed suspicious and
hostile. He could be tender toward people, but he had turned his
back utterly on what he had left behind.

Newman's ability to value what was true in the views of other
Christians did not, however, make him blind to difference. It is
the second credential. In his *Apologia*, while he spoke plainly of
his reluctance "to cause offence to religious Anglicans," he admitted he felt bound all the same to confess his "astonishment that
I had ever imagined [the Church of England] to be a portion of
the Catholic Church." It reads as a sharp rebuff. He acknowledged
its outstanding qualities as an institution, its wisdom, its political
power, its place in the nation's life, and its witness to and teaching
of religious truth, but he could no longer see it as "something sacred." "It may be a great creation, though it be not divine, and this
is how I judge of it" (*Apo.*, 339–342 [296–298]). Understanding
of the Church, of course, has developed since those days. Newman did not have at his disposal the nuanced recognition, supplied by the Second Vatican Council's Decree on Ecumenism, of
a communion between separated Christians that is real though
imperfect (*Unitatis Redintegratio*, no. 3). In his day, the lines were
drawn more starkly.

All the same, while Newman could be forthright about the difference between the Catholic position and that of others, he was
not blind to Catholic defects, which is the third credential identified by Dessain. In his journal in 1863, he spoke of his conviction
that "the Church must be prepared for converts, as well as converts prepared for the Church" (*A.W.*, 258). And fourteen years
later, in 1877, he expressed forcibly the difficulty he saw. "It is so
ordered on high," he wrote in his preface for the third edition of
his *Lectures on the Prophetical Office*, "that in our day Holy Church
should present just that aspect to my countrymen which is most

consonant with their ingrained prejudices against her, most un-promising for their conversion" (*V.M.* i, xxxvii [23]). This realism about the Church implied recognition of what was true and to be valued among others, as well as what was defective among Catholics. Moreover, it is an example I have tried to follow.

When my book *The Catholic Faith* first appeared in 1986, it was reviewed on BBC Radio Ulster. The reviewer observed:

> Dr. Strange approaches his task with a candor that apologists for other Christian traditions would do well to imitate. Self-criticism in religious writing is like the bitter lemon that brings out the flavor in good fish. So Dr. Strange does not hesitate to meet head on nastiness wherever he finds it . . . throughout these pages the author is, if anything, prepared to err on the side of ecumenical generosity. [7]

I appreciated then, and do so now, these kind words, which, I would add, once more bear witness to Newman's influence. Nevertheless, the reviewer reserved a sting for the tail. "For all that," he added, "a real Catholic heart beats beneath the veneer of benign ecumenism."[8] I am proud of my Catholic heart but long to overcome the suspicion suggested by that final phrase. How might it be done? And here the fourth credential comes into play, the desire to offer a complete and balanced account of Christian truth.

Exploring Newman's life and thought has already raised for us a number of issues that sometimes have been seen as controversial. Liberalism in religion pointed to the possible tension between dogma and theology. There were those who saw dogma always as dogmatizing, an assault on the freedom to think, which is essential for theology; and there were those who viewed theology as lacking focus or definition. Newman, however, championed dogma when it was threatened but sought to safeguard freedom for theology when it was not. Then again, papal infallibility was feared by some as the gateway to doctrinal tyranny, while it was eulogized by others who tried to extend its boundaries. Newman, as we noticed, placed it in a larger context, seeking to calm fears and clip the wings of extremists. Then there were some who could make no sense of the place of the laity in the Church; for them they were simply "boys eternal." Newman, on the other hand, viewed their situation very differently. Driven by his commitment to education, he wanted to equip them for the role they needed to play. On each occasion, he tried to avoid extremes and offer an account on which people could agree and around which they could unite. For us it is not a matter of agreeing with each particular position he took. We may, or we may not. More important is his strategy—an attractive, gentle handling of contentious issues that seeks to clarify misunderstandings so that they may be overcome. Nevertheless, even this strategy is not everything. Something more is needed.

Consider another testing area for ecumenical discussion— Mary, the Mother of the Lord. The Anglican-Roman Catholic International Commission produced its document *Mary: Grace and Hope in Christ* in 2004. Newman explored such matters in his *Letter to Pusey* in 1866. Here, too, he followed his customary path by trying to moderate extremism, clarify misunderstandings, and present an account on which all could agree. We have already seen the substance of what he had to say,[9] but there is a rarer, more particular lesson to be learned from that controversy. It touches the very heart of ecumenical discussion and emerges from an awareness of the circumstances that led to it and the conditions in which it took place. It makes for an intriguing story.

(iii)

On September 12, 1865, Newman visited John Keble, his friend and counterpart in the Oxford Movement, in Keble's vicarage at Hursley. The visit had been planned for some time, but at the last moment, he almost decided not to go because he heard that Pusey was by chance visiting the same day. The three of them had not met for about twenty years, and he felt it might all be too much at last to see both of them together. But then he thought better of it, he felt he was being cowardly, so he turned up unannounced. The visit went well. They talked for four or five hours and had dinner together, something they must have done often in the past in Oriel at high table or with other friends, but, Newman noted later, extraordinary as it may seem to us, it was "the first and last time in their lives" that they had dined together "simply by themselves" (*L.D.* xxiv, 142; *L.D.* xxii, 51–53).

The following month news of their meeting became known. It was reported in the press that Pusey and Newman had been reconciled. Pusey was offended and wrote to the editor of the Tractarian newspaper, the *Guardian*, on October 9 to correct the very idea that reconciliation could ever have been called for. "The deep love between us," he declared, "which now dates back for above forty years, has never been in the least overshadowed. His leaving us was one of the deep sorrows of my life; but it involved separation of place, not diminution of affection."[10] This declaration of his bond with Newman set the scene for what happened next.

At the time of their meeting, Pusey had become embroiled in a controversy with Manning, who had just been named Archbishop of Westminster. Manning, in a public letter to Pusey, had reacted to a popular view that had identified him as one of those Roman Catholics who were, in a phrase of Pusey's, "in an ecstasy of triumph" over certain troubles within the Church of England. He wanted to set the record straight. His pamphlet, though not unsympathetic, was marked by his characteristic vigor and directness, rejoicing in the workings of the Holy Spirit within the Anglican Church but unable to "regard the Church of England as 'the great bulwark against infidelity in this land.'"[11] Pusey, challenged, felt called to answer Manning's charges, but he also saw the exchange as an opportunity to promote the reunion of the Christian Church. He named his reply *An Eirenicon*.[12]

During his conversation with Newman and Keble, Pusey was full of this work, and at the time Newman had neither the desire nor the inclination to become involved. In fact, he and Pusey had already discussed the matter by letter. Ten months earlier Newman had remarked, "Of course I do not see things on your side sufficiently to be able to say that you should not answer [Manning]— but I am tempted to ask, Why should you?" (*L.D.* xxi, 315).

One part of Pusey's approach was to draw up a list of Roman excesses in devotion to Mary, such as the views that while Jesus in fact gained us our salvation out of obedience to his Father, he could have won it out of deference to his Mother,[13] and that, as well as the Christ, it is Mary who is present and received in the eucharist.[14] When his book appeared, reviewers were appalled. R.W. Church, the future dean of St. Paul's, a highly influential position in the Church of England, and a friend of both Pusey's and Newman's, expressed his revulsion in the *Times*: ". . . there is something absolutely bewildering, like the imaginations of a sick dream, in this audacious extravagance of dogmatism, unfolding itself inexhaustibly into ever stranger and more startling conclusions."[15] This revulsion, of course, was the very reaction that Pusey wished to arouse among Catholics, in the hope they would dismiss the extravagance and so make reconciliation easier and more likely. Newman had no doubt that his plan had misfired.

At first he was silent. He was disappointed because he felt that Pusey had exaggerated. He believed that his unbalanced presentation of Roman practices was only going to make matters worse. Pusey made no attempt, he pointed out to Keble, "to soften the impression he leaves on the reader, of the *universality*" of extreme views held by people like Faber. He made such views seem common to all. "The whole tone," Newman declared, "is antagonistic" (*L.D.* xxii, 91–92). He finally wrote to Pusey himself at the end of October and admitted his disappointment. He told him: "An Irenicon smoothes difficulties; I am sure people will think that you increase them" (*L.D.* xxii, 90).

Pusey, of course, was pained by Newman's reaction. He did not wish to appear hostile under the guise of speaking peace. He tried to illustrate his case by using serious authors, and he told Newman, "I thought, 'There it is; if any of it is disowned, it is a gain.'"[16] Newman wrote back the following day, November 5, reassuring Pusey that his intention had not been lost on him, but he feared that most people would miss that point and settle down to the parts they could understand more easily (*L.D.* xxii, 93). He also mentioned that at that time he still had no intention of publishing anything himself, but he promised him that if he did, it would be in the spirit of an eirencon, in the cause of peace.

They continued to exchange letters, Pusey gently but firmly pressing his case, while Newman replied frankly and directly. Keble feared their relationship might cool. "I do hope he [Newman] will not waver in his friendship for you," he remarked to Pusey.[17] The fear was unfounded. At the very time of disagreeing with him, Newman was also writing to Pusey enthusiastically, offering to help with the French translation of his book and advising him to delay its publication so that he could take into account any comments from Manning (*L.D.* xxii, 102), while Pusey wrote wondering whether Newman "could draw up something which I might put before the English Church, as firm to offer."[18] They were very cordial disputants.

On November 24, Newman had still not finally decided to join the debate, but four days later he left for Rednal, the Oratorians' house in the country outside Birmingham, to prepare his response.

(iv)

Newman was moved to write at last by more than the need to answer Pusey. He also felt keenly the harshness of Rome's dealings with Catholic members of the Association for the Promotion of the Unity of Christendom. Membership had been prohibited the previous year, and an appeal by 187 Anglicans had led only to a condemnation of a branch theory of the Church. Such events created the impression that all Catholics were as extreme as Faber and Ward (*L.D.* xxii, 110). Newman wished to qualify that impression. He wanted to answer Pusey without causing him pain (*L.D.* xxii, 112), and he hoped also, as we have seen earlier, that if he confined his remarks to the Mariological section, he might supply an alternative to the Mariological excesses of writers like Ward and Faber, which created such an obstacle for others. That was why he stated in his published *Letter* that he wanted people to know, "did they come to stand where I stand, what they would, and what they would not, be bound to hold concerning [the Blessed Virgin]" (*Diff.* ii, 25).[19]

At Rednal, Newman wrote at great speed. He also sent letters to both Keble and Pusey on December 8, the feast of the Immaculate Conception, so that they knew what he was doing. He stressed to them his wish not to cause pain and his desire to preserve the eirenical spirit (*L.D.* xxii, 118–119). Pusey replied the next day. The controversy had gathered momentum, and he was relieved that Newman was taking part. He noted: "This discussion is taking too wide a range, for me to wish you to be silent."[20] And indeed Newman wrote eirenically, true to his conviction that "Abuse is as great a mistake in controversy, as panegyric in biography" (*L.D.* xxii, 211).

It is not surprising that Newman was able to write so fast. He was on familiar ground, throwing parts of his *Essay on Development* into more popular form and distilling ideas he had expressed previously in private letters. He explained the difference between Faber and Ward, on the one hand, and himself, on the other, and tried to make clear the distinctions between doctrine and devotion and between intercession and invocation. He also repudiated foreign extravagance as "a bad dream," "calculated to prejudice inquirers, to frighten the unlearned, to unsettle consciences, to provoke blasphemy, and to work the loss of souls" (*Diff.* ii, 113–115). His *Letter* was published on January 31.

After publication, Keble wrote within days, gracious as ever, and Pusey wrote soon afterward. He too was grateful, especially for Newman's kind words about himself, but all the same he took the opportunity to explain various points he disputed. And so the controversy continued. Both men received praise and rebuke from their own communions as well as from each other's. Pusey went on to write two further volumes of *Eirenicon*, both addressed as *Letters* to Newman, while Newman eventually continued his reply to Pusey, almost ten years later, when he responded to Gladstone's views about authority and the papacy in his *Letter to the Duke of Norfolk*. Their business remained unfinished.

(v)

The outcome of this exchange may well seem disappointing. It had so much to commend it. It is, after all, relatively rare for two people who enjoy so close and affectionate a friendship to be locked in public debate, disagreeing sharply but without acrimony. Moreover, as we have seen, their friendship meant they were able to discuss their separate positions in private letters as well as by the exchange of their published works. And then the sympathy between them seemed to create the most favorable climate for resolving their disagreement satisfactorily. Yet the progress they made was slight. Indeed, at the end they did not really seem any closer than they had been at the beginning. Why? Two reasons in particular explain.

First, it may well be that the very understanding of the Church that they employed defeated them from the start. Newman held to the claim of the Roman Catholic Church to be exclusively the Church of Christ, while Pusey worked with the branch theory of the Church with all the complexities and questions that such a view involves. Also, although both desired reunion, they were prompted to write for different motives. Pusey wanted to answer the charges leveled by Manning, while Newman in addressing Pusey was concerned primarily to make public and establish openly an English disposition to certain Catholic doctrines and devotions that at that time were suffering from an excessive amount of continental color and influence. In the circumstances, it is hardly surprising that their exchanges were not more fruitful. Were they, therefore, a waste of time? Have they nothing to teach us so many years later? Not necessarily.

One sentence from this controversy has become famous. At the beginning of his public *Letter*, Newman took Pusey to task for calling his book *An Eirenicon*. "There was one of old time," he remarked, "who wreathed his sword in myrtle; excuse me— you discharge your olive-branch as if from a catapult" (*Diff.* ii, 7). Henry Liddon, Pusey's friend and biographer, acknowledged the turn of phrase but called it unjust for it "cleverly diverted attention from the fact that the sting lay in the obstacles themselves and not in their enumeration."[21] R.W. Church, on the other hand, reviewing Newman's *Letter* in the *Times* on March 31, 1866, agreed wholeheartedly with Newman: "This is, no doubt, exactly what Dr. Pusey has done."[22] Such reactions are instructive.

Liddon's meaning is plain enough. In fact, Church's was essentially the same. He was arguing that Pusey had no alternative but belligerence. He had given more credit to Rome than most people would have thought possible, and so it was necessary to state the obstacles also, openly and courageously. Church was pleased that Newman had detached himself from these obstacles, the extravagances of the extremists, but he went on to observe, "it seems to us much more difficult for him to release his cause from complicity with the doctrines which he dislikes and fears." Church then identified the crucial issue, the question "whether [Newman] or the innovators represent the true character and tendencies of their religious system?"[23]

It is a telling point that cuts to the very heart of ecumenical discussion. It is not answered by making distinctions between doctrine and devotion, invocation and intercession, however necessary and proper those may be in their place. Whether Pusey was inaccurate at times in his exposition makes little difference. He had articulated a suspicion and aroused a prejudice, and Church's reaction bore witness to it. All their sympathy and friendship— for Church too was a close friend—could not erase that element of uncertainty. How could it be overcome? The only antidote to suspicion in these circumstances was a more widespread, popular trust. It was possible to believe Newman. But was he really able to speak for the others?

At the very least, therefore, this dispute between Pusey and Newman is a cautionary tale. It illustrates how hard ecumenical discussion can be. The whole episode is a warning that the "agreed statements" on our shelves, on the eucharist, ministry, and authority, on the nature of the Church, Mariology, and justification by faith, and on many other subjects besides, will count for little, even combined with love, sympathy, and friendship for individuals, unless there also exists among us an unequivocal trust that reaches out widely and is deeply felt. And even then progress may well be slow.

(vi)

Newman's final Anglican sermon, "The Parting of Friends," was preached on September 25, 1843. It was the sermon heard by the grandfather of the woman who showed me Newman's home in Littlemore on my first visit.[24] His penultimate sermon, however, at least among those that were published, he preached earlier that year at Pentecost. He spoke about the link within the Church between what is personal and what is public. "We cannot hope for unity of faith," he remarked, "if we at our own private will make a faith for ourselves in this our small corner of the earth." It is not difficult to imagine the pressure he must have been feeling at that time as he wrestled with his situation and struggled to come to a decision. Should he remain an Anglican or turn to Rome? Was the Church of England a faith wedded to its small corner of the earth, or was its scope larger? His dilemma is visible between the lines of the text, and so it comes as no surprise to hear him describe "the division of Churches" as "the corruption of hearts" (*S.D.*, 133). His distress is evident.

More than twenty years later, debating with Pusey, he was still working to overcome that division. And the manner in which he worked, valuing the good, stating differences, acknowledging defects, and presenting a balanced account of the issues, on the one hand, while, on the other, remaining faithful in love and friendship, sympathy and trust, offers us a path to follow. What better way to heal the corruption of hearts? And if the outcome for Newman in this instance was disappointing, it does not prove he was mistaken. It only shows us that the road he faced was rough, but still it was and remains the right road.

8

Strange Providence

(i)

Newman kept a journal for most of his life. As the years went by, he added to it only occasionally. The entry for June 25, 1869, was the first for more than six months. It began: "The Providence of God has been wonderful with me all through my life" (*A.W.*, 267). Various reflections on the ways of providence follow, and they include references to the outcome of the three illnesses he suffered earlier in his life: the first, in boyhood, bringing him to Christianity; the second, as a young Oxford don, leading him to break with liberalism; and the third, as he said, "in 1833, when I was in Sicily, before the commencement of the Oxford Movement" (*A.W.*, 268).

This view of his experience in Sicily as providential had been fixed in his mind from the start. He began his account of it in August 1834 with the words "I seem to see, and I saw, a strange providence in it" (*A.W.*, 121). Newman, like most of his contemporaries, had a keen sense of providence. He was to describe it years later as "nearly the only doctrine held with a real assent by the mass of religious Englishmen" (*G.A.*, 57 [44]). In any case, no student of his life and work could doubt its importance for him. We have seen already how he described the Church of England as "the instrument of Providence" in conferring benefits on him (*Apo.*, 341 [297]).[1] And his return to Sicily without his friends in 1833 stood out in his mind as a further powerful example of providence at work in his life. But this whole idea of providence can cause bewilderment today.

It is commonly understood simply as God's plan for us. Good luck or a happy coincidence we sometimes describe as providential. But that may lead to seeing it as God's intervening, imposing something on our lives that changes the natural course of events. We have obvious difficulties with such a notion, God as the grand chess master in the sky, moving us about like pawns on the board. If divine providence refers to God's plan, it needs also to refer to something more. So how is this doctrine to be understood? Newman's experience in Sicily seems to me to offer clues. It certainly helped me shape the account I gave in my book *Living Catholicism*, where I explained it not only as God's plan for us, but as involving also God's presence; and plan and presence, if they are to become providential, require of us perception as well.[2] We need to look more closely at what happened to Newman, and it will help us get to know him better.

(ii)

He spoke of his solitary return to Sicily as "a strange providence" (*A.W.*, 121). The adjective can have various meanings. What is strange can be foreign, alien, hostile. Again, as a bearer of the name, a victim of countless puns and unoriginal jokes, I know to my cost it can be used as a synonym for what is odd or peculiar. And it can also mean something that causes surprise, amazement, and wonder. In that sense, Lord Byron called truth "stranger than fiction,"[3] and in the same sense, I suggest, Newman found his Sicilian adventure strange. The ways of providence took him by surprise, amazed him, caused him to wonder. Remember what happened.

After the tutorial dispute with Provost Hawkins at Oriel, Newman had been deprived of pupils, and so he was free to take a Mediterranean voyage with his friend Hurrell Froude and Hurrell's father, the Archdeacon of Totnes. During the trip, as arranged, they visited Sicily and from there went on to Rome. But then Newman had a fresh idea. He found Sicily enchanting. He longed to see it again. So, while his friends went back to England through France, he, regardless of them and contrary to plan, decided to retrace his steps. After a while, however, he became dangerously unwell, probably with typhoid fever. He came to see his own behavior as an example of the very willfulness against which he had preached in Oxford the day before setting off on this holiday. At the same time, he felt with growing confidence a sense of vocation in his returning to England because he was convinced that God had a work for him to do.

What account can be given of the ways of providence in this experience? The plans of providence are commonly recognized only with hindsight. It might be asked, what was God planning for Newman in Sicily? Was it the stimulus to return to England on fire with a sense of mission? That might seem the natural answer. But Newman himself saw in this second, unplanned visit to the island an act of willfulness. Did God sow the willful seed? That would make matters more complicated. We must proceed with care. One of the most confusing and least helpful features in the discussion of providence is the tendency to identify every aspect of what takes place as some particular divine intervention. That leads people into supposing, for example, that it was God who prompted Newman to leave his friends and return willfully to Sicily so that there in a lonely place he could strike him down with a dangerous illness and thereby reform his life and reveal to him his mission. We have to unravel the threads. We can begin with Newman's idea of willfulness.

(iii)

In his memoir written in 1834, Newman saw the strange providence of his illness as a judgment and a punishment. It was a judgment on him, he believed, because he felt he had received the eucharist unworthily, owing to the resentment he still felt toward Edward Hawkins, the provost of Oriel, over the tutorial dispute. It was a punishment, he said, "for my willfulness in going to Sicily by myself" (A.W., 121). He had reported his awareness of his willfulness already. It occurred in his earliest written account of his experience, the letter he sent to his friend Henry Wilberforce a week after his return. He explained that he came to feel God's fighting with him. He went on:

> I came to think that there was some willfulness in my coming to Sicily, as I did. . . . And then I felt more than I had done the willfulness of my character generally. . . . And then I recollected that the very day before I left Oxford, I had preached a University Sermon against willfulness, so that I seemed to have been predicting my own condemnation. (L.D. iv, 8)

This reference to his sermon, "Willfulness, the Sin of Saul," is intriguing (U.S., 156–175). It is not as straightforward as it may seem. In the sermon, willfulness is always a sin, while Newman told Wilberforce that, although he became aware of having sinned, he had been comforted in his illness by a sense of not having brought the situation on himself by going against advice and by the phrase that had come back to him and that he had repeated often, "I have not sinned against the light." So Newman's allusion to his willfulness may be explained more naturally as characteristic of someone whose view of himself is at a low ebb. He may not have sinned gravely, but he had been stubborn. His return to Sicily seemed to have lacked consideration for his friends. As he observed: ". . . though no one had advised me against it, yet I fancied I ought to have discovered they thought it an over-venturous thing" (L.D. iv, 8). Certainly it was marked by his determination to do what he wanted to do. These features of his visit match well his description of willfulness in the sermon as "the unaccountable desire of acting short of simple obedience to God's will, a

repugnance of unreserved self-surrender and submission to Him"
(*U.S.*, 161). Newman's return to Sicily may not have involved serious sin—he was not sinning against the light—but his behavior
was flawed by mixed motives. And then he fell ill.

To understand the working of providence as Newman perceived
it in the light of his Sicilian visit, it is essential to remember that
there was no trace of his wrestling with God, his brooding on his
failings, or his dark judgment of himself until the illness struck.
Here was the strange providence, the cause of surprise and wonder. His perilous condition brought about a revelation of divine
presence. His declining fortunes in Oxford, his resentment at the
provost, the general state of fatigue that had led him to join the
Froudes for this holiday may all have combined, even in him whose
sense of God's presence was so vivid, to dull his awareness of that
presence. The illness revived it.

It was a crisis whose effects were spiritual as well as physical.
Suddenly he saw the obstacles that had troubled him since leaving the Froudes in Rome—presumably the difficulties and delays
that had beset his return to the island—as signs of God's fighting
against him. He recognized the poor manner of his behavior over
the tutorial dispute and the way his resentment of the provost
had, as he judged it, made his reception of the eucharist unwor-
thy. And in his very journey to Sicily, he discovered a particular
example of the general willfulness that, he concluded, marred his
character. He indulged his own will too much. He seemed at least
to resemble Saul, who had "preferred his own way to that which
God had determined" (*U.S.*, 164). Here he was lacking that unreserved self-surrender and submission to the divine will he urged
upon others. Nevertheless, in spite of these hazards, his resistance
to God and his willfulness, he felt comforted even in the depths
of his sickness. He was comforted, he told Wilberforce, because
he had not gone against any advice he had actually received and
because of his sense he had not "sinned against the light." And
then, he added, "I thought I would try to obey God's will as far
as I could" (*L.D.* iv, 8). What a strange providence indeed to have
been so preserved from serious sin and then enlightened by grave

illness. On his way home on June 16, becalmed at sea, Newman poured his feelings into three brief stanzas.

For many years congregations have delighted in singing "Lead, Kindly Light," largely oblivious of its origins (*V.V.*, 156–157). To know its source, the relief and gratitude that inspired it, is to recognize instantly its intense personal character for Newman and to understand why he could not bear to hear it sung in his own oratory in Birmingham. It captured poignantly his experience of the kindly light that had guided him through darkness when he was far from home: one step was enough; it acknowledged the willfulness that once had loved to see and choose its own path, but now no longer; it professed hope in the power that would continue to guide him over rough countryside of every kind—moor and fen, crag and torrent—till the night was gone and there remained only angel faces and perfect love.

The reflections in Newman's letter to Wilberforce, in his memoir, and in his poem followed very closely upon the experience itself. They are too immediate for a clear view of this strange providence to emerge. His understanding of that can be seen better by complementing his account with his observations about providence in later years. Sicily was never mentioned, but its influence is unmistakable.

(iv)

Consider first the sermon "Divine Calls," which Newman preached on October 27, 1839 (*P.S.* viii, 17–32). He took as his text a verse from the First Book of Samuel: "And the Lord came, and stood, and called as at other times, Samuel, Samuel. Then Samuel answered, 'Speak; for Thy servant heareth'" (1 Sm 3:10). He drew from it the lesson of prompt obedience to the call and added a number of other examples: David, Paul, and various apostles, on the one hand, the rich young man and various waverers, on the other, all of whom, by their acceptance or refusal, illustrated the same lesson. The characteristic of divine calls, he concluded, was "to require instant obedience" (*P.S.* viii, 22). Remembering Sicily, we hear these words as a reproach to that willfulness that acts "short of simple obedience to God's will" (*U.S.*, 161). And he went on at once in the sermon to notice that divine calls "call us we know not to what; [they] call us on in darkness" (*P.S.* viii, 22), which seems to echo his poem: "The night is dark, and I am far from home – / Lead Thou me on!" (*V.V.*, 156).

Next, the sermon reflects on the many calls that people receive throughout their lives, from sin to repentance, from grace to grace, from holiness to holiness. People who live religiously, Newman explained, "have from time to time truths they did not know before, or had no need to consider, brought before them forcibly: truths which involve duties, which are in fact precepts, and claim obedience." These are occasions when Christ is calling them, they are particular moments, and yet in themselves they are unexceptional. He observed: "There is nothing miraculous or extraordinary in His dealings with us. He works through our natural faculties and circumstances of life." And this divine action, carried out in everyday ways, Newman spoke of as providential: "Still what happens to us in providence is in all essential respects what His voice was to those whom He addressed when on earth" (*P.S.* viii, 24). How well this description captures the pattern of that strange providence that overtook Newman in Sicily: a lesson learned afresh about obedience to God's will through the suffering of an ordinary, although serious, illness.

The image of his experience in Sicily as an implicit influence was reinforced when Newman went on to remind his congregation about the way in which these calls occur. They are commonly sudden and unexpected. He mentioned how a letter, a message, or a person can provide a trial, which, "if met religiously," can be the means of bringing someone to a high state of knowledge and holiness. An unexpected illness would have been an apt example. Crises force us to take stock. He stressed further that he was not speaking of cases in which people change their whole lives or reverse their opinions and conduct. Outwardly they remain much as they were, just like himself after Sicily, we may add; but inwardly they have entered into "a new world of thought," and they measure things and persons "by a different rule," again, just as he had done (*P.S.* viii, 25–26).

   There is no self-evident claim that this sermon was conceived intentionally as a commentary on his illness in Sicily, but even what someone forgets can influence his or her imagination, and the view of providence he presented here dovetails noticeably with that experience. It would be more surprising if it did not. His illness was providential. But there was more to the providence than that event alone. Perhaps the key remark about these calls was his observation that "We are slow to master the great truth, that Christ is, as it were, walking among us, and by His hand, or eye, or voice, bidding us follow Him" (*P.S.* viii, 24). Providence is at work among us not merely as a plan, but also through presence. The ordinary outward event is recognized as providential when the divine presence is perceived within. There are two layers and they combine.

(v)

   Two years later, in 1841, Newman turned again to the question of providence when he reviewed Henry Hart Milman's *History of Christianity*. If the emphasis in the sermon could be said to favor the event or plan within which the presence is discerned, the review lays stress rather on the presence that is at work within the plan. At first it might not seem so. Newman stated: "Now it has ever been a firm article of Christian faith, that [God's] Providence is in fact not general merely, but is, on the contrary, thus particular and personal." The reference to the particular and personal may seem to suggest intervention, the intrusive outward event. But Newman at once continued: ". . . as there is a particular Providence, so of necessity that Providence is secretly concurring and co-operating with that system which meets the eye, and which is commonly recognized among men as existing." Providence operates within the ordinary. He then laid down what he called "the one great rule" for God's relationship with the human race and creation: "the visible world is the instrument, yet the veil of the world invisible,—the veil, yet still partially the symbol and index: so that all that exists or happens visibly, conceals and yet suggests, and above all subserves, a system of persons, facts, and events beyond itself" (*Ess.* ii, 192). We hear the chord of romantic Platonism being firmly struck, the conviction that, as symbols participate in the reality they symbolize, so the visible world veils a world unseen.[4] Newman declared: "All that is seen,—the world, the Bible, the Church, the civil polity, and man himself,—are types, and in their degree and place, representatives and organs of an unseen world, truer and higher than themselves." He allowed that there was a distinction to be drawn: some things may seem to be more obviously supernatural or symbolical, while others seem to be complete in themselves, or may even seem opposed to the unseen system that in fact they serve and support (*Ess.* ii, 193). But all that is, along with so much that occurs, whether evident or not, is the veil and vehicle of the divine presence.

"When Providence would make a Revelation," Newman observed, "He [God] does not begin anew, but uses the existing system": Priests give us his blessing, the elements of this world are used to consecrate us and give us life, divine order follows a natural form. Even miracles are worked, he remarked, "without superseding the ordinary course of things." He gave as examples the increase of Jacob's flocks and descendants and their deliverance from Egypt, and concluded: "But still the operation of ordinary causes, the influence of political arrangements, and what is called the march of events, are seen in such providences as truly, and can be pointed out as convincingly, as if an Angel or a pillar of a cloud were not with them" (*Ess.* ii, 194). The precritical coloring of these observations makes their content all the more telling. And although unmentioned, his experience in Sicily was a natural illustration of this teaching. These words express so well what happened to him. Everything that took place, leading up to his illness as well as the illness itself, was entirely explicable by natural causes; yet it brought about a revelation of God's presence that flooded his being, convinced him of his recovery, and instilled in him a sense of mission. As he told Henry Wilberforce: "I could not help saying, I must act as if I were to die, but I think

God has work for me yet" (*L.D.* iv, 8). Here, once again, we are led to the conclusion that in providence, plan and presence combine; outward event and inward reality are one.

So far, so good, perhaps. We can set aside the shallow notion that providence is God's acting in an intrusive, manipulative way. Events that are providential have natural causes. We have seen, moreover, that God is always present and that it is the inner reality of his abiding presence that makes what takes place providential. But now we may discover a fresh difficulty. If God is always present, in what sense is providence particular? This emphasis on his abiding presence seems to empty the teaching on providence of any distinctive content. Something further needs to be said. We must investigate more deeply. We can do so by turning to a slightly earlier sermon, preached in 1835 and called "A Particular Providence as revealed in the Gospel" (*P.S.* iii, 114–127).

(vi)

Drawing on a wide range of biblical examples, from Balaam to Judas, Newman developed this theme. God is good and everyone is in his presence. All the same, crises occur as that presence is neglected or forgotten. This, he said, "is often the state in which persons find themselves on falling into trouble. The world fails them, and they despair, because they do not realize to themselves the loving-kindness and the presence of God" (*P.S.* iii, 117). Their fortunes begin to change when they rediscover that presence. The rediscovery makes it seem like a new truth, and it is that rediscovery that is providential. "Some especial Providence," he noted, "amid their affliction, runs right into their heart, and brings it close home to them, in a way they had never experienced before, that God sees them." This surprise brings delight and can even sweep them to the opposite extreme, making them suppose that they are loved more than others. They are mistaken. There is a "particular Providence over all" (*P.S.* iii, 118). Everyone is loved by God individually. In a passage, memorable for me because of the impression it made on me when I first read it, Newman evoked this humbling and awe-inspiring truth:

> God beholds thee individually, whoever thou art. He "calls thee by thy name." He sees thee, and understands thee, as He made thee. He knows what is in thee, all thy own peculiar feelings and thoughts, thy dispositions and likings, thy strength and thy weakness. He views thee in thy day of rejoicing, and thy day of sorrow. He sympathizes in thy hopes and thy temptations. He interests Himself in all thy anxieties and remembrances, all the risings and fallings of thy spirit.

There is much more, but at the core we find the declaration "Thou dost not love thyself better than He loves thee" (*P.S.* iii, 124–125).[5] What more could we ask?

The account of providence that emerges in these writings teaches that it operates on three levels, or is composed of three dimensions. First of all, God is indeed at work. He is acting in the particular and personal way that is appropriate to each individual. Providence, for Newman, is not just a turn of phrase. He believed that God has a plan that is being fulfilled. Its action is not interference. It is a part of the ordinariness of everyday life, its laws, its sequence of cause and effect. Second, the inner reality of this plan is God's abiding presence within all his creation. Living in that presence and responding to that plan, whether by acceptance or refusal, is the very nature of the human condition. But the particular feature that makes a situation providential is a third element, the recognition by the individual of the divine presence within the events that are taking place. What we designate as providential are those moments or occasions when we become aware of God's will for us. They are privileged perceptions of his abiding presence.

Once again, we may detect Newman's experience in Sicily behind this teaching because it illustrates it so well. His illness was a strange providence. Although intelligible in natural terms, Newman saw it nonetheless as a particular event through which he came to recognize afresh God's presence to himself and thereby came also to know his will. Plan, presence, and perception coincided.

This teaching has value still. Of course, it may disappoint those who think simplistically of providence as divine intervention. They may feel bewildered or become angry when life is hard; they want God to intervene and solve their difficulties. Divine power, however, is not like that, a merely superhuman power; and God's providence, as Newman implied, is not an occasional, intrusive, manipulative presence but one that remains with us both in tragedy and joy. Moments we recognize as providential are like sacraments of God's love. They are the times when we perceive more clearly God's plan for us, as well as his love as an abiding and present reality.[6]

(vii)

Newman's experience in Sicily was so powerful it seems natural to wonder how long its impact endured.

In the *Apologia*, Newman described his return to England in nervous, staccato sentences (*Apo.*, 35 [43]). Father Henry Tristram, who first edited Newman's autobiographical papers at the Birmingham Oratory long after Newman had died, noted how they conjured up, even after thirty years, the "mental tension under which he labored" (*A.W.*, 119). Yet on to the next page, beginning a new section, Newman commented disarmingly, "I soon relapsed into the every-day life I had hitherto led" (*Apo.*, 36 [44]). The intensity of the moment was not maintained; that was hardly to be expected. Nevertheless, the effect did endure.

Newman acknowledged that he was "in all things the same, except that a new object was given me" (*Apo.*, 36 [44]). He was referring to his sense of a new mission and the part he was to play in the Oxford Movement. That too passed in time. But what seems never to have ended, however much the experience may have faded, was his renewed sense of the intimate, personal presence of God. What impressed him in his youth and perhaps became jaded by bereavement, disappointment, and fatigue was restored in Sicily and never left him. Its effect can be detected in a meditation that was published only after his death. It speaks of his part in God's plan, and it can also speak to us:

I am created to do something or to be something for which no one else is created; I have a place in God's counsels, in God's world, which no one else has; whether I be rich or poor, despised or esteemed by man, God knows me and calls me by name.

God has created me to do Him some definite service; He has committed some work to me which He has not committed to another. I have my mission—I never may know it in this life, but I shall be told it in the next. Somehow I am necessary for His purposes, as necessary in my place as an Archangel in his . . . I have a part in this great work; I am a link in a chain, a bond of connexion between persons. He has not created me for naught. I shall do good, I shall do His work; I shall be an angel of peace, a preacher of truth in my own place, while not intending it, if I do but keep His commandments and serve Him in my calling.

Therefore I will trust Him. Whatever, wherever I am, I can never be thrown away. If I am in sickness, my sickness may serve Him; in perplexity, my perplexity may serve Him; if I am in sorrow, my sorrow may serve Him. My sickness, or perplexity, or sorrow may be necessary causes of some great end, which is quite beyond us. He does nothing in vain; He may prolong my life, He may shorten it; He knows what He is about. He may take away my friends, He may throw me among strangers, He may make me feel desolate, make my spirits sink, hide the future from me—still He knows what He is about. . . .

I ask not to see—ask not to know—I ask simply to be used. (*M.D.*, 399–402)

A sense of the divine presence, of purpose and plan, breathes through this passage. Its prayerful conclusion, "not to see" but "to be used," echoes his poem "The Pillar of the Cloud," which he composed when becalmed on his journey home, and marks it as a fruit of that strange providence that overcame him on his Sicilian journey.

9

Preaching a Living Faith

(i)

Newman landed in England after his Mediterranean journey on July 8, 1833. He was back in Oxford the following evening, and six days later, July 14, John Keble preached the Assize Sermon, which expressed alarm at what he saw as government intrusion into the rights of the Church of England. Newman always regarded it as the start of the Oxford Movement. There was a meeting soon afterward to consider the issues Keble had raised, but Newman was not there. In any case, as we know, he was impatient with such gatherings. In his view, "Living movements do not come out of committees," (*Apo.*, 39 [46]). Soon he began the series of short pamphlets that gave the Movement its other name, Tractarian. But even they were not the main source of his influence at that time. He exercised that from the pulpit in the University Church.

Imagine, therefore, that it is about five minutes to four one Sunday afternoon in Oxford in the late 1830s. You are an undergraduate, and as you usually do, you are walking briskly with a group of your friends across Broad Street, down the Turl, and into Radcliffe Square, eager to reach the University Church by four o'clock. Your college has moved the hour of its evening meal so that it clashes with the service in an attempt to dissuade you and your friends from going to St. Mary's at that time, but that maneuver has, if anything, only fueled your enthusiasm to attend. You reach the church and take your place in one of the pews. You try to pray but feel distracted as you wait for the preacher to arrive. You are waiting for John Henry Newman.

In old age you will look back on those Sunday afternoons as golden memories. Your thoughts may echo Matthew Arnold's:

> Forty years ago, when I was an undergraduate at Oxford, voices were in the air there which haunt my memory still. Happy the man who in that susceptible season of youth hears such voices! they are a possession to him for ever . . . the name of Cardinal Newman is a great name to the imagination still, his genius and his style are still things of power. But he is over eighty years old. . . . Forty years ago, he was in the very prime of life; he was close at hand to us at Oxford; he was preaching in St. Mary's pulpit every Sunday; he seemed about to transform and to renew what was for us the most national and natural institution in the world, the Church of England. Who could resist the charm of that spiritual apparition, gliding in the dim afternoon light through the aisles of St. Mary's, rising into the pulpit, and then, in the most entrancing of voices, breaking the silence with words and thoughts which were a religious music—sweet, subtle, mournful? I seem to hear him still . . . .[1]

What was it that Arnold would have heard? What would you have heard? According to Stephen Dessain, it was a balanced exposition of the Christian gospel as revealed religion, the cause that gave Newman's life its unity.[2] So those who listened at St. Mary's each Sunday would have heard teaching on the three persons in the one God; on the Incarnation, death, and resurrection of Jesus; on salvation; on the indwelling of the Holy Spirit; on the Church; on the sacraments; on holiness; on sin and forgiveness; and on much else besides. It is not possible, of course, to present everything here, but let me try to give the flavor at least of what you and those who went with you to St. Mary's during those momentous years would have heard by presenting some aspects of his account of faith.

This subject, of course, preoccupied Newman on many occasions, notably in his formal *Oxford University Sermons*, in his *Grammar of Assent*, and in the various papers he wrote to hammer out his thought over the years. That material has created a minor industry for philosophers of religion, but I am not planning to add to it unduly here. My concern is more with Newman's pastoral sermons, those sermons where, as Owen Chadwick once remarked, the Oxford Movement's best writing was "enshrined."[3] My choice is not arbitrary. Nevertheless, to set the scene, I am going to begin elsewhere.

(ii)

Toward the end of *A Grammar of Assent*, we find one of those phrases that does more than state Newman's point of view; it helps define him as a person. He declares, "if I am asked to convert others by [a smart syllogism], I say plainly I do not care to overcome their reason without touching their hearts" (G.A., 425 [273]). I mentioned this quote earlier.[4] Newman wanted always to speak to the heart. It became his motto as a cardinal, "Heart speaks to heart—*Cor ad cor loquitur*." And yet when we consider his preaching, this statement may at first seem inconsistent.

When Newman preached at St. Mary's, he tended to avoid direct controversy, but he was also offering in his account of the gospel a clear alternative to the viewpoints proposed by his evangelical and liberal contemporaries. They too, however, as he admitted, appealed to the heart. His sermon "Self-Contemplation," preached in 1835, referred to evangelical impatience with dogma, which he, of course, condemned; his disapproval is unsurprising.

But then he went on to mock its insistence on "a certain state of heart": "they lay it down as self-evident, that the main purpose of revealed doctrine is to affect the heart," so that what does not affect it may safely be rejected or dismissed as relatively unimportant (*P.S.* ii, 166–168). But wasn't he intent on touching hearts as well? And at the end of the previous year, he preached on "The Gospel, a Trust Committed to us." Here he discussed the liberals, those he called "the reasoners of this age." He argued that they failed to unfold the mysteries of the gospel and concentrated instead on analysis, considering creeds merely as "fetters on souls." At the same time, however, for them too, "the great end of the Gospel is the union of hearts in the love of Christ and of each other" (*P.S.* ii, 259–261). Once more there is this emphasis on the heart. Again, wasn't that his own preoccupation? So was Newman being inconsistent? We need to look more closely.

What he criticized was the view, shared by evangelical and liberal alike, that a doctrine's effect on the heart was the primary test of its significance. Newman's religion of the heart was never a religion of the heart in that sense. He preached a revealed religion, and the heart had its place, not as a criterion of significance, but so that what was revealed could be recognized as real by those who heard him and come alive for them. He wanted to engage the heart, to kindle in people a living faith, that sensitivity to mystery that he once described as "colorless, like air or water; it is but the medium through which the soul sees Christ; and the soul as little really rests upon it and contemplates it, as the eye can see the air" (*Jfc.*, 336). Sitting in St. Mary's Sunday after Sunday, you would have learned much about this response to revelation, about the nature of a life lived by faith.

(iii)

One of Newman's earliest sermons was called "Religious Faith Rational," and he preached it on May 24, 1829 (*P.S.* i, 190–202). What makes this particular one interesting is the way he was already adopting at that time the approach that was to become so characteristic of him later—eschewing theory and settling for empirical observation. In particular, he emphasized that believing and trusting were inevitable.

He was dismissive of the idea that faith and trust were confined to religion: "we are acting on trust every hour of our lives," he remarked. He gave the examples of our memory and our powers of reasoning. "And what I wish you particularly to observe," he went on, "is, that we continually trust our memory and our reasoning powers in this way, though *they often deceive us.*" If in daily life our continued trust in our memory and reason, despite errors, does not make us irrational or credulous, then neither should it do so in religion, for "When faith is said to be a religious principle, it is (I repeat) the things believed, not the act of believing them, which is peculiar to religion" (*P.S.* i, 191, 192). To believe, to trust, is not only possible for human beings, it is unavoidable.

Next he took the argument a stage further. Remarking that reliance on memory or reasoning powers might be seen as no more than trust in ourselves, he went on to illustrate that reliance on another, on testimony, which is integral to religious faith, is an everyday experience as well. We acknowledge the existence of towns we have never seen, and writing, of course, long before satellite photography, he referred to the way the British accept that they live on an island, though they have never toured the coastline. We are convinced, he declared, by "the *report of others.*" And he commented that this faith in testimony is called irrational only "when religion is concerned." And he concluded that scripture "only bids us act in respect to a future life, as we are every day acting at present" (*P.S.* i, 195). We are guided by faith.

One reason for the interest in this sermon is the way it anticipates his approach in *A Grammar of Assent*, which he published forty-one years later in 1870. There, too, Newman insisted on the human constitution as a principle and starting point: "If I may not assume that I exist, and in a particular way, that is, with a particular mental constitution, I have nothing to speculate about, and had better leave speculation alone" (*G.A.*, 347 [224]). The example that Great Britain is an island also finds a place in the argument (*G.A.*, 294–296 [191–192]), but it is worth noting that

Newman's misgivings about his earlier arguments as an Anglican hardened. His view that "it may be said . . . that to trust our senses and reason is in fact nothing more than to trust ourselves" (*P.S.* i, 193) became a "reluctance to speak of our trusting memory or reason, except indeed by a figure of speech." Why? "It seems to me unphilosophical," he explained, "to speak of trusting ourselves. We are what we are, and we use, not trust our faculties" (*G.A.*, 61 [46]). In other words, his later, more explicit adherence to the principle of working from the human constitution revealed the weakness or inappropriateness of those particular illustrations. It had not, however, affected the conclusion that human beings, whether religious or not, necessarily live by faith.

In his 1829 sermon, Newman introduced a further dimension, namely the reason for trusting in God. Belief is not only something natural to human beings and based on testimony, which in this particular case meant the witness of others that sacred scripture comes from God. Newman declared: "We obey God primarily because we actually feel His presence in our consciences bidding us obey Him" (*P.S.* i, 200). The authority of the Bible derives from God, perceived through conscience. At this early date, Newman was already placing specific emphasis on the role of conscience. He was to write about it at length in the *Grammar* (*G.A.*, 105–118 [73–81]) and to preach on it with memorable power and beauty in Dublin on the Fourth Sunday of Advent in 1856 (*O.S.*, 64–66, 74), but it was a prominent theme in his *Parochial Sermons* as well. You would have heard him mentioning it on various occasions as you sat listening each week. There was a sermon he called "Faith without Sight," which he preached on St. Thomas's Day, December 21, 1834. In fact, it was the forerunner of the Dublin sermon.

In a compact passage, Newman made three closely linked points. First, he identified those who are religious as those who are attentive to "the rule of conscience." Conscience, he explained, is born with them but not devised by them. It is distinct. And the religious person "feels bound in duty to submit" to it. Second, therefore, conscience points a person beyond himself: it "immediately directs his thoughts to some Being exterior to himself, who gave it, and who evidently is superior to him." It follows from that sense of being duty-bound to submit, "for a law implies a lawgiver, and a command implies a superior." And third, there is a fine interweaving of what is external and what is interior. "Thus," Newman went on,

> a man is at once thrown out of himself [*external*], by the very Voice which speaks within him [*interior*]; and while he rules his heart and conduct by his inward sense of right and wrong, not by the maxims of the external world [*interior*], still that inward sense does not allow him to rest in himself, but sends him forth again from home to seek abroad for Him who has put His word in him [*external*] . . . He looks out of himself for the Living Word to which he may attribute what has echoed in his heart [*external and interior*]. (*P.S.* ii, 18)

To live by faith is to live in obedience to conscience. The voice of conscience alerts the believer to the authority on which that faith rests.

There is similar teaching in another sermon, "Faith without Demonstration," which Newman first preached on May 21, 1837. There, too, he argued against those who sought rational proof for belief. He maintained that we commonly trust the opinions of others—for example, in legal matters—without becoming experts ourselves. We rely on authority. So it is not unreasonable to do the same in religion. And to the objection that the law of the land is not improbable or difficult, while, for instance, the Catholic teaching on the Trinity is mysterious and unlikely, Newman replied that that is just what we should expect: "I do not say that it *is* true, *because* it is mysterious; but if it *be* true, it cannot help being mysterious" (*P.S.* vi, 333). And he pursued the point further. In the end, however, he acknowledged that the Being of God cannot be proved. There may be much to impress us, to strengthen us in faith, to encourage devotion, but the unbeliever will not be moved to faith by strict, formal evidence. It does not have that power. Instead, Newman urged, we must learn to walk by faith, and he returned to the role of conscience:

> There is a voice within us, which assures us that there is something higher than earth. We cannot analyze, define, contemplate what it is that thus whispers to us. It has no shape or material form. There is that in our hearts which prompts us to religion, and which condemns and chastises sin. And this yearning of our nature is met and sustained, it finds an object to rest upon, when it hears of the existence of an All-powerful, All-gracious Creator. It incites us to a noble faith in what we cannot see. (*P.S.* vi, 339–340)

In these sermons, therefore, Newman was arguing for the reasonableness of faith, not by supplying some incontrovertible logical proof, but by pointing to the trust that is common among human beings and our reliance on authority. At the same time, he indicated the authority upon which religious faith rests by appealing to the way conscience alerts us to God's existence and the reality of his presence. That may be its basis. What, however, is its reality? In what does religious faith consist?

(iv)

For Newman an essential part of the answer to that question identified faith with obedience. He preached on that topic in 1830 and declared: "To believe is to look beyond this world to God, and to obey is to look beyond this world to God, to believe is of the heart, and to obey is of the heart; to believe is not a solitary act, . . . and to obey is not a solitary act. . . ." He acknowledged that faith and obedience stand for different ideas in our minds but asserted that in fact they are "but one thing viewed differently" (*P.S.* iii, 80–81). The relationship between faith and obedience was a regular theme in his sermons (*P.S.* viii, 201–216; *P.S.* v, 166, 183–184), but these two are woven together in a way that rewards particular study in his sermon "Saving Knowledge." It was composed early in 1835, as the Oxford Movement, then barely eighteen months old, was beginning to gather momentum. It is set down as a sermon for Easter Monday.

The "saving knowledge" of the title is the knowledge of God, revealed in the flesh, Jesus Christ, the incarnate Lord. But if the knowledge of God is eternal life, how are we to know that we know him? That was the question Newman raised. What assurance do we have that we are not mistaken or in a dream? Some Christians, he observed, believed their faith to carry with it its own evidence. He was not convinced so easily. He quoted St. John: "Hereby do we know that we love Him, if we keep His commandments" (1 Jn 2:3), and commented: "Obedience is the test of Faith." He saw these two, faith and obedience, as "the whole duty and work of the Christian" (*P.S.* ii, 153).

Then he referred to the kind of teaching, which we discussed earlier, that was dismissive of doctrine and regarded doing good "as a mere cold and formal morality," while it insisted instead on "a spiritual state of heart" (*P.S.* ii, 154). But Newman insisted on faith and obedience, obedience as evidence of faith. He had in mind general obedience, not just one good quality or another. There is some good in everyone. But the habit of obedience is necessary. "The more we *do*, the more shall we trust in Christ" (*P.S.* ii, 160). Obedience leads to faith and then becomes its fruit and guarantee.

This insistence on obedience may be rare nowadays. Some years ago in Oxford, I planned to preach on it and called in at a local bookshop that was well stocked with theology. "Have you got anything on obedience?" I asked. With a smile I was told, "Nobody's writing about obedience these days." Yet for the Christian, obedience is not about a regulated response to a command, but instead it is about a life lived in fidelity to the demands of the gospel. For an illustration of such fidelity, we need to look no further than Newman himself, not the relatively young man at the height of his influence in Oxford who was preaching these sermons, but the man he became more than thirty years later, not yet a cardinal, who could survey a life shredded by disappointments. It is the story with which we have become familiar.

He had had his hopes for the Church of England overturned, and his reception into the Catholic Church had brought about a sorrowful parting from many of his dearest friends. He had responded generously to various invitations but then had been let down: his efforts to found the University in Dublin had been constantly thwarted; his plans to translate the Bible had been allowed to evaporate; his attempt to support the *Rambler* by taking over as editor had been undermined; his hopes for an oratory in Oxford had been systematically frustrated. It comes as no surprise to find that entry in his journal in 1863, when he had been brought so low, where he gave vent to his feelings:

> O how forlorn and dreary has been my course since I have been a Catholic! . . . since I made the great sacrifice, to which God called me, He has rewarded me in ten thousand ways, O how many! but He has marked my course with unintermittent mortification . . . since I have been a Catholic, I seem to myself to have had nothing but failure, personally. (*A.W.*, 254–255)

He was all too familiar with disappointment and a sense of being defeated. His spirits may have been lowered; nevertheless, as the gratitude expressed in his journal showed, he remained faithful.

(v)

Central to Newman's understanding of Christian discipleship was his refusal to concentrate on any one virtue or quality exclusively. The sermon on saving knowledge was careful to avoid the pitfall that assumed that a single good quality could be the guarantee of true holiness. General obedience, many qualities together, make up the whole. On February 25, 1838, as you listened, you would have heard Newman speaking about the relationship between faith and love.

There is a sense, he suggested, in which love is "all virtues at once." It is the material "out of which all graces are made." He described it as a quality of mind, a disposition, in other words, that is the fruit of new life in Christ. Those who are newly born in Christ are rooted in love. And the Spirit dwells in that love. "Faith and hope are graces of an imperfect state, and they cease with that state; but love is greater, because it is perfection" (*P.S.* iv, 309). Love is "the seed of holiness, and grows into all excellences, not indeed destroying their peculiarities, but making them what they are" (*P.S.* iv, 311). "Faith is the first element of *religion*, and love, of *holiness*; and as holiness and religion are distinct, yet united, so are love and faith" (*P.S.* iv, 312). "Moreover, it is plain," he went on,

> that, while love is the root out of which faith grows, faith by receiving the wonderful tidings of the Gospel, and presenting before the soul its sacred Objects, the mysteries of faith, the Holy Trinity, and the Incarnate Savior, expands our love, and raises it to a perfection which otherwise it could never reach. And thus our duty lies in faith working by love. . . . (*P.S.* iv, 314–315)

There is much more packed into this sermon that handles so delicately this life-giving relationship, but let us break off at this phrase, "faith working by love"; in effect, *fides charitate formata*.

Let us suppose that your enthusiasm for Newman is such that not only do you attend his weekly sermons in St. Mary's, but the previous year, 1837, you also heard his *Lectures on Justification*, delivered in the Adam de Brome Chapel in the University Church. That phrase, "faith working by love," might well have stirred in your memory one of those lectures' most captivating passages. Newman declared:

> I would treat of faith as it is actually found in the soul; and I say it is as little an isolated grace, as a man is a picture. It has a depth, a breadth, and a thickness; it has an inward life which is something over and above itself; it has a heart, and blood,

and pulses, and nerves, though not upon the surface. All these indeed are not *spoken* of, when we make mention of faith; nor are they painted on the canvas; but they are implied in the word, because they exist in the thing. . . . Love and fear, and heavenly-mindedness, and obedience and firmness, and zeal, and humility, are as certainly one with justifying faith, considered as a thing existing, as bones, muscles, and vital organs, are necessary to that outward frame of man which meets the eye, though they do not meet it. Love and fear and obedience are not really posterior to justifying faith for even a moment of time, unless bones and muscles are formed after the countenance and complexion. It is as unmeaning to speak of living faith, as being independent of newness of mind, as of solidity as divisible from body, or tallness from stature, or color from landscape. As well might it be said that an arm or a foot can exist out of the body, and that man is born with only certain portions, head or heart, and the rest accrues afterwards, as that faith comes first and gives birth to other graces. (*Jfc.*, 265–266)

The virtues weave together to form a seamless web of holiness.

(vi)

If we next ask how Newman viewed the condition of a person in whom these qualities and virtues have come together, we can turn to the beginning of his sermon "The State of Salvation." He preached it on March 18, 1838, which was only six days after he had finished preparing his *Lectures on Justification* for publication. He contrasted someone enslaved to sin and filled with darkness to a person in whom the blessings of Christ have found their home. "As that which is created differs from what is not created," he observed, "so the Christian differs from the natural man. . . . As far as a being can be changed without losing his identity, as far as it is sense to say that an existing being can be new created, so far has man this gift when the grace of the Gospel has its perfect work and its maturity of fruit in him" (*P.S.* v, 178–179). No greater contrast could be imagined. New life in Christ, living faith, brings about what has been called a share in the divine nature. In a Christmas sermon, Newman set out this teaching plainly:

> Men we remain, but not mere men, but gifted with a measure of all those perfections which Christ has in fullness, partaking each in his own degree of His Divine Nature so fully, that the only reason (so to speak) why His saints are not really like Him, is that it is impossible—that He is the Creator, and they His creatures. . . . (*P.S.* viii, 253)

This is the doctrine of divinization, proclaimed in scripture (2 Pt 1:4) and expounded by the fathers of the Church.

All the same, it would be a mistake to presume that this privileged condition was a panacea. For Newman the contrary was closer to the truth. Soon after he described the state of salvation in such exalted terms, he preached a sermon that was one of his most moving. It displayed notable psychological perceptiveness. It was called "Sins of Infirmity."

On this occasion Newman indicated that the results of faith "are righteous and holy," but he also acknowledged, "the process through which they are obtained is one of imperfection." From a distance, he remarked, the soul of the righteous appears "youthful in countenance, and bright in apparel; but approach him, and his face has lines of care upon it, and his dress is tattered." His righteousness has been "wrought out of sin, the result of a continual struggle,—not spontaneous nature, but habitual self-command." And he went on:

> True faith is not shown here below in peace, but rather in conflict. . . . As we gain happiness through suffering, so do we arrive at holiness through infirmity, because man's very condition is

a fallen one, and in passing out of the country of
sin, he necessarily passes through it." (*P.S.* v, 210)

Those who "venture much with their talents," he added a little
later, "gain much . . . [but they] cannot believe that they are making any progress; and though they do, yet surely they have much
to be forgiven in all their services. They are like David, men of
blood; they fight the good fight of faith, but they are polluted with
the contest" (*P.S.* v, 214).

These few sentences can convey only slightly the effect of the
whole; still, they may be enough to show that Newman did not
regard believing as offering immunity from conflict. Indeed, in
1836, you would have heard him urging you to seek out conflict,
when he told you that, as faith is the essence of a Christian life,
so there is a duty "in risking upon Christ's word what we have, for
what we have not" (*P.S.* iv, 299). We need to make what he called
"ventures of faith," and what I, in part through learning from him,
have described elsewhere as "the risk of discipleship." We must
be prepared to make a commitment and accept the consequences
whatever they may be, consequences that are not of our choosing.
What virtue is there in living in such a way that it would make no
difference to us if Christ's word proved to be false?

(vii)

This chapter may have been more demanding, more difficult
than the others, but the earlier chapters will, I hope, have prepared the way for it. I have tried to offer something substantial
for reflection by presenting this account of Newman's teaching on
faith as it appeared in his pastoral sermons. And we have caught
glimpses of his spirituality as well.

At the start it was important to appreciate the circumstances
of those times that influenced what he had to say, evangelicalism and liberalism, while it was also necessary to be aware of the
convictions that guided him as a preacher, especially his devotion
to religion as revealed. We have found him attentive to human
experience so that his words would be real, his sermons come

alive. We have seen the emphasis he placed on faith as common to everyone, not something peculiar to the religious, and on the part played by witness and testimony. We have also considered the role of conscience as the authority within us, pointing us beyond ourselves. And we have heard his account of the bond between faith and obedience, and not only obedience, but the other virtues as well that are woven together, a seamless robe, an entire disposition that establishes us in a privileged condition before God, which gives us indeed a share in the divine nature and which bestows on us perfection at the last, but which at first is experienced as conflict. We must be prepared to take risks for Christ's sake. There should be much in this teaching that can speak to us still.

Earlier, I compared your memories to Matthew Arnold's. Let us return to him once more.

Arnold seemed to have heard a passage from a sermon called "Peace in Believing." Newman preached it first in May 1839. He offered comfort, the reward of a living faith:

> After the fever of life; after wearinesses and sicknesses; fightings and despondings; languor and fretfulness; struggling and failing, struggling and succeeding; after all the changes and chances of this troubled unhealthy state, at length comes death, at length the White Throne of God, at length the Beatific Vision. (*P.S.* vi, 369–370)

Now, it has been suggested that Arnold in fact would have heard Newman only rarely, but that matters little to us. Rather the contrary. For, if it is true, the vividness of his memory reveals the power of the impression the preacher made on him. And we know that such impressions are not commonly composed out of theory. Arnold's clear memory bears witness to the reality of Newman's experience.

10

Witness to Holiness

(i)

For twelve years it was my good fortune to be one of the Catholic chaplains at Oxford University. During that time, whenever I said Mass in the chaplaincy, I celebrated it in a chapel dedicated to St. Thomas More. There was, however, one exception. At eleven in the morning on Sundays, especially during the school year, that chapel could not accommodate the numbers that came, and so Mass was celebrated in the large hall. It was called the Newman Room. For those years, therefore, that central act of my ministry as Catholic chaplain was celebrated in a place associated with either More or Newman, two Englishmen acclaimed by many for their holiness. My particular concern here, of course, is with Newman, but in considering his witness to holiness, it will be helpful to keep an eye on Thomas More as well, noticing what he and Newman had in common as well as where there were contrasts.

More, for example, has been described as born for friendship, yet we know he loved solitude and retained throughout his life a sympathy for the Carthusian vocation, which he had tried as a young man. And Newman, as we have seen, wrote in 1829 of the "Blessings of friends, which to my door, unask'd, unhoped, have come" (*V.V.*, 46), yet he was also said to be never less alone than when alone. In 1868 he even commented: "I have often been puzzled at myself, that I should be both particularly fond of being alone, and particularly fond of being with friends" (*L.D.* xxiv, 53).

Then there is the irony of the contrast between their public and private faces. More is fixed in the popular imagination as a man of wit, satire, and good humor, a merry man; people tend to forget the darker, more pessimistic side. Newman, on the other hand, is generally thought of as humorless, austere, and forbidding; however, as we have noticed before, he could be funny, and often too in ways reminiscent of More—dry wit, satirical perception, and a deadpan humor that could leave people unsure whether there was a joke.[1] I think, for instance, of the reservation he expressed in a letter in 1877 about an Anglican sermon of his because it contained the phrase "the Church has erred." The phrase, he said, grated on him. He quipped, "I should not mind 'the Pope has erred'" (*L.D.* xxviii, 274). Again, Thomas More was devoted to education. Public life may have limited his contribution to humanist studies, but his place in the new learning is assured. And Newman, as we have seen time and again, was devoted to education; it was "his line," one of the major concerns that governed his life. And then there was conscience, which Newman famously would toast before toasting the pope (*Diff.* ii, 261) and to which More adhered, maintaining thereby his communion with the pope, although he was in fact no extreme ultramontane, and thereby losing his life.

Friendship and solitude, humor and gravity, education and conscience, these are some of the threads that bind these two men to each other. But my main concern is with holiness, and here their paths may seem to diverge, one a martyr, the other dying peacefully in his bed. But before we consider the contrast, we should remember what holiness entails.

(ii)

Christian holiness must never be diminished to an abstraction. We must look steadily at Jesus of Nazareth, that man, his life, and learn from him. We call him Savior, and in the past it has been common to locate his saving work in his crucifixion: Jesus saved us by dying on the cross. More recently, however, the part played in our redemption by the resurrection has been restored. And more than that, we must acknowledge the significance of the birth of the Christ as well, and his hidden life, and his public ministry. In other words, the significance of Jesus of Nazareth can never be reduced to the events of a particular Friday afternoon. His birth, his hidden life and public ministry, his death on the cross and resurrection to glory are all of a piece. The entire sequence of events is salvific because it gives expression to something else, something interior, something within.

Jesus of Nazareth was the faithful one. His whole existence was shaped by an interior disposition of perfect love and obedience. He loved his heavenly Father and was obedient to his will; he loved all men and women and was obedient to, at the service of, their need: because of sin, they needed to be saved. It was the Father's will that he minister to that need. There was a perfect correspondence in his obedience. Jesus was faithful.

To place such emphasis on interior disposition should not lead us to neglect the external events. The human condition is a unity composed of both. There is a fine interweaving. Interior reality has external consequences. It is vital to realize that our salvation was achieved not because Jesus mindlessly followed a prearranged program of events that led to his crucifixion but because he was utterly faithful to the Father's will and our needs, and so he accepted the consequences of that fidelity, however terrible they might have been. So when the gospel speaks of holiness and urges us to be Christlike, it is not imposing on us trials and sufferings, arbitrarily conceived, but encouraging us to develop an interior life that equips us for the testing that will follow. Testing is the inevitable consequence of this kind of fidelity, fashioned within, in a sin-scarred world.

The life and death of Jesus were of a piece. But at once we realize there is a distinction that has to be made. He, the Word made flesh, may have given us an example of perfect fidelity, but that cannot be expected of us. We know all too well that our lives do not display that consistency. There is always a need for growth, and there will be a crisis. Given that each one's pilgrimage is unique, these two elements—of growth and of crisis—seem to be the most common. And here More and Newman offer a striking contrast.

(iii)

Thomas More obviously had a crisis; he was martyred. But where, it might be asked, was the growth? Was he not, in Erasmus's famous phrase, the title of Robert Bolt's play, "a man for all seasons," outstandingly well-rounded and well-integrated? But if those words are understood as abstracting him from his own season, then they do not do him justice. He cannot be removed from his own time and place. Nobody can. He was not so much a man for all seasons as a man for every season, because he was a man of his own season, deeply involved in the issues and demands of his day. We should admire him not because he somehow held himself aloof from them but because, while he struggled with them, he was not absorbed by them. He was not at their mercy. He felt the call of solitude but longed also to be married; he wrestled with his desire for scholarship but was drawn to the demands of his professional life; he studied and understood the truth about the nature of the Church, although throughout his life its appearance was largely unlovely; and he recognized the implications of the king's great matter, his divorce, and stood firm to resist them.

I am not suggesting that Thomas More swept along some high road of supreme virtue, untouched by compromise, misgiving, or failure. Nobody does that. The famous wit could wound as well as make merry; the polemical pamphlets, salted with scatology and relentless invective, hardly accord with an image of saintliness; he was ambitious; and he persecuted heretics with zeal. He would have understood without difficulty Newman's remarks that "True faith is not shown here below in peace, but rather in conflict" and that "in passing out of the country of sin, [man] necessarily passes through it" (*P.S.* v, 210). More limped along often enough. If he can be honored as a saint, however, it is not merely by turning a blind eye to his failings or because he was martyred. We are not required to like the language of the pamphlets or applaud the persecution of heretics. Thomas More is a saint because he grew in holiness. He struggled with the choices placed before him. Then, when his time came to die, he was prepared. His death was of a piece with what had gone before. He had worked to fashion his fidelity from the complexities and ambiguities of his own experience.

What, however, are we to say about Newman?

(iv)

If Thomas More is remembered especially for the crisis of his martyrdom, Newman is remembered especially for development, not only of doctrinal theory, but of the personal journey. Let me recall briefly the main moments that by now are familiar enough.

Born in 1801 and brought up in an Anglican home with a thorough knowledge of the Bible, he underwent a kind of evangelical conversion when he was fifteen. Its effects lingered for some years, but as a young fellow of Oriel in 1822, in a common room that was said to stink of logic, he came under the influence of Richard Whately, sturdy logician, eccentric character, and future Anglican Archbishop of Dublin. He drew Newman out of his shy shell, and through Whately, Newman was touched by Oriel's rationalism. But soon he was affected still more by other friends, notably Hurrell Froude, Edward Pusey, and John Keble. Their friendship, his own illness in 1827, and the death of his sister Mary in 1828 brought him to recognize the limitations of intellectual excellence alone. Then in 1833, responding to what he and his friends saw as a crisis within the Church of England, he preached and lectured and campaigned with them to arouse in his fellow Anglicans a keener sense of their own heritage within the Catholic tradition. By 1841, however, the understanding of the Anglican Church that he had advocated seemed to him to have been repudiated.

He was on his "death-bed" in the Church of England from that time. On October 9, 1845, after immense soul searching, he was received into the Roman Catholic Church. Newman had moved from evangelicalism through rationalism into a perception of the Church of England as Catholic and then on from there to Roman Catholicism. He had been growing; he had been on pilgrimage.

At the same time, it is important to realize that this movement was not evidence of restlessness for its own sake but a consequence of his tireless search for the fullness of Christian truth. As a Catholic too he probed the great mysteries of faith, and anyone who knows Newman well will acknowledge the truth of his remark to an evangelical correspondent, George Edwards, to whom he wrote in 1887. He was eighty-six at the time. He spoke of "those great and burning truths, which I learned when a boy from evangelical teaching" and which he had "found impressed upon my heart with fresh and ever increasing force by the Holy Roman Church" (*L.D.* xxxi, 189). Newman's thought developed but remained also remarkably consistent. He was a pilgrim, not a religious wanderer. But was he a saint?

"By their fruits you shall know them." It is a wise test of sanctity. The fruits of Newman's work have been considerable. His writings have touched vast numbers of people. Many of his sermons have a power still, which time has not dimmed. His influence on religious thought has been wide-ranging. His *Essay on the Development of Christian Doctrine* in 1845, imperfect and, indeed, unfinished as it was, opened an area vital for the Church's self-understanding. Since the Second Vatican Council, a stream of books and articles has appeared arguing that Newman had anticipated ideas that the Council had emphasized, for example, on the papacy, the laity, and on ecumenism, and there are deeper currents as well.[2] The fruits of his work have been extensive. All the same, people are not canonized simply for their writing. When Newman himself is considered as a man, two main criticisms tend to be expressed.

(v)

First of all, he is thought to have been too sensitive. In his dealings with people, he seems to have been extremely touchy. The suggestion has often been made that whether it was Oxford colleagues, fellow Oratorians, or Church authorities, he took offense far too easily and could be waspish in reply. Various comments can be made. On the one hand, I suspect that Newman's own clarity of thought made him a rigorous critic of even passing remarks, which at times lent those remarks a weight they were never intended to carry. He may not always have been the most comfortable person with whom to live. Then, on the other hand, the charge of excessive sensitivity, offered as a bar to sanctity, falls into the trap of implying that only people with certain temperaments can truly be holy. Obviously that will not do. There are no privileged or handicapped temperaments. Holiness is available to all: it depends on the way we handle the raw material.

The second criticism is more serious. In effect it argues that when Charles Kingsley wrote, "Truth, for its own sake, is not a virtue with the Roman clergy. Father Newman informs us that it need not, and on the whole ought not to be," he was in a way right. Most obviously, of course, he was wrong, but the suspicion lingers that he had pointed to a real weakness. If that suspicion has any basis, then I suggest it has to do with a problem common among intellectual people. Those who are skillful at marshaling arguments may well be in danger of being able to present a case so effectively that a false position may pass as true. It is almost an occupational hazard for the intellectual.

For the sake of argument, therefore, let us suppose that Newman was as hypersensitive as people have sometimes suggested, and let us suppose that his very gifts of mind made him a prey to the hazards of advocacy. We can then learn two lessons about holiness. First, that if a person is a saint, that does not mean he or she has always been so. As Newman himself observed, even among the greatest saints, there are those who "in early life were committed to very un-saintly doings" (*H.S.* ii, 341). It is the point with which this book began, the point echoed by Pope Benedict

XVI when he observed, "Holiness does not consist in never having erred or sinned."[3] The discovery of some failing, even serious, is no necessary disqualification from holiness. Newman, like Thomas More, had failings he had to struggle to overcome.

More seriously, however, the attitude that regards a person who has sinned as incapable of holiness is dangerously mistaken. There is a danger because, although sinning is not essential to being human, it is in fact inescapable (without the privilege granted to the Mother of Jesus, but that is another question). It follows that to identify holiness with sinlessness is either to make it altogether unattainable or to remove it from the realm of ordinary human life. It is ironic that the very people who say, "Thomas More isn't a saint; he persecuted heretics," or "Newman cannot be canonized; he was shifty," are the same people who would be most opposed to that uncritical attitude to the saints that we call hagiography, while their standpoint implies that, if holiness ever were achieved, it could only be of a kind that would invite that extreme hagiography they most deplore. We need to be clear. We can become holy, even though we have sinned and maybe sinned grievously. We do so not by suppressing our humanity, but by bringing it, after much struggling, whole and entire, into a harmonious relationship with the Spirit of Christ, which dwells within us. We grow into holiness and accept the consequences.

It is clear, then, that Newman was a pilgrim. He grew in holiness. But he died in old age, a cardinal of the Roman Church, held in high esteem by his countrymen. Where, it might be asked, was the crisis? Was there a crisis? The gospels tell us that there has to be, because "Whoever does not bear the cross and follow me cannot be my disciple" (Lk 14: 27). How many of us hear those words and wonder about them? What cross do we bear, you and I? In Thomas More's case, the cross was evident. He was martyred. But what about us? What about Newman?

(vi)

Years ago, when I was first ordained and people came to see me in distress, because of illness, because a husband or wife had died, or because their career plans had been disappointed and their gifts frustrated, I used to see them as exceptions. That was partly because I was young and partly because I had been fortunate. Experience soon taught me otherwise. Virtually everyone has to face crisis, often more than one. Crises are like defeats. They have no relieving features. It is never good to be handicapped, for a loved one to die, for people to be unemployed, for gifts to be squandered. It may be, in fact, that those who are handicapped accept the challenge of their disability and give an outstanding example of courage, that the bereaved person remarries happily in due course, that talents acquired are not wasted in the end, but the sense of defeat at the time is nonetheless devastating. It is a crucifixion. These people are as defeated in these ways as Jesus was on Calvary. We must not take advantage of the hindsight Easter supplies. Jesus had been perfectly faithful to his Father's will; he had spent himself in love for everyone; yet his love was rejected, and his ministry lay in ruins. The essence of crucifixion is not wood and nails but defeat.

Newman's life offers us many examples. We have become familiar with them. His hopes for the Church of England were rejected, and his reception into the Catholic Church brought about a terrible parting from many of his closest friends: Keble's letter, asking for forgiveness for a seventeen-year silence, is particularly moving (*L.D.* xx, 501–502). And then there were those enterprises of his Catholic years, the founding of the university in Dublin, his translation of the Bible, the invitation to edit the *Rambler*, and his hopes for an oratory in Oxford; his plans and efforts seemed always to be undermined and frustrated. And there were the clashes as well with people like Manning and Faber and W. G. Ward. He knew himself to be an object of pity and contempt. By the early 1860s, his days were dark, and it comes as no surprise to read that entry in his journal in 1863 that we have noted before. It is instructive to see it again in this context:

> O how forlorn and dreary has been my course since
> I have been a Catholic! . . . since I made the great
> sacrifice, to which God called me, He has rewarded

me in ten thousand ways, O how many! but he
has marked my course with almost unintermittent
mortification . . . since I have been a Catholic, I
seem to myself to have had nothing but failure,
personally. (*A.W.*, 254–255)

Newman knew intimately that defeat that lies at the heart of crucifixion, and his dark hours can alert us to recognize when we
too are being tested. Everyone goes through such a crisis. And if
it arouses intense self-pity, then the defeat can smother us and
will indeed be death-dealing. But if a person can somehow remain generous, open-hearted, loving, even at such a time, then it
is possible to move on from disaster to new life.[4] In these times of
crisis, when defeat seems heaviest, fidelity is the key. As Jesus even
on Calvary commended himself into his Father's hands, so was
he raised from the dead. We find that same vital steadfastness in
those who seek holiness.

Thomas More's son-in-law, William Roper, recorded for us
More's remark at their parting, "Son Roper, I thank our Lord, the
field is won," words that Roper understood to mean that "it was
for the love he had to God wrought in him so effectually, that it
conquered in him all his carnal affections utterly."[5] And we may
remember how Newman, after suffering and withstanding so
many disappointments, particularly as a Catholic, learned finally
that he was to be made a cardinal. That, of course, was only a human judgment, but it lifted from his name and from his writings
the insidious, damaging suspicion that his views were unreliable,
unsound. As he told his old friend Mother Mary Imelda Poole: "It
is a wonderful Providence, that even before my death that acquit-
tal of me comes, which I knew would come some day or other,
though not in my life time" (*L.D.* xxix, p. 63). He had been proved
wrong.

(vii)

The way Thomas More died is well known. He was beheaded
on the scaffold. His composure, his grace, his good humor did not

desert him, as he waited for the ax to fall. He died "in and for the faith of the Holy Catholic Church."[6] He died a martyr. The manner of Newman's death is less well known. Father William Neville, Newman's secretary and caregiver in his later years, described his final days.

On August 9, 1890, he explained, Newman came into his room, and his step was at first unrecognized, it seemed so firm and elastic; and he was "unbent, erect to the full height of his years in the fifties." His carriage was "soldier-like, and so dignified; and his countenance was most attractive to look at; even great age," Neville remarked, "seemed to have gone from his face, and with it all careworn signs; his very look conveyed the cheerfulness and gratitude of his mind, and what he said was so kind; his voice was quite fresh and strong, his whole appearance was that of power, combined with complete calm. . . ."[7] However, he became ill that night with congestion. He got up the next morning, but he had to return to bed later, and the following day, August 11, at about a quarter to nine in the evening, he died. He had been unconscious for most of the day.

The gentleness of his passing makes a vivid contrast with the violence of More's. Yet both of them had striven for fidelity. One died on the scaffold, the other in bed, but both had nourished their interior lives to grow in holiness and been confronted by external crisis. By remaining faithful they had turned victory into defeat, passing from death to new life. As a younger man, Newman had already expressed the matter most simply: "The planting of Christ's Cross in the heart is sharp and trying; but the stately tree rears itself aloft, and has fair branches and rich fruit, and is good to look upon" (*P.S.* iv, 262).

11

The Flame of Love

(i)

When the news broke that Newman had died, tributes poured that bore witness to the esteem in which he was widely held throughout the country. As we have seen, it had not always been like that. Forty-five years earlier, when he had left the Church of England and become a Roman Catholic, many of those whom he left looked upon him with contempt, while those whom he had joined, the small Catholic community, lacking in self-confidence, were unsure how to use his gifts and regarded him with suspicion.

This combination of contempt and suspicion gradually led to forgetfulness and neglect until, nineteen years later, Charles Kingsley casually accused him of indifference to the truth. The injustice of that charge in particular Newman found insupportable and, as we know, it provoked the correspondence that caused him to write his *Apologia pro Vita Sua*, through which he described the steps that had led to his conversion to Catholicism. He was vindicated triumphantly, as old friends acknowledged the honesty of his actions and, moreover, were surprised and moved to discover the continuing warmth of his affection for them, while new friends began to recognize the caliber of his gifts. As we have seen, it was one of the great turning-points in his life. It restored to him the respect of many that had been lacking for so long.

Thus restored, early the following year, in January 1865, he felt compelled to write again. The subject was very different. He has described his mood: "On the 17th of January it came into my head to write it. I really cannot tell you how, and I wrote on till it was finished, on small bits of paper. And I could no more write anything else by willing it, than I could fly" (*L.D.* xxii, 72). What he was writing in this way was his long poem "The Dream of Gerontius." It seems fitting to draw these reflections on Newman to a close by exploring some aspects of this poem about death and judgment. It is a kind of coda.

(ii)

"The Dream of Gerontius" tells of the death of a man of faith who has lived life to the full. He is a good man but not a saint. To put it simply, Gerontius has been saved; he will go to heaven; but first he must be purified. There is a purgatory for him to undergo. In Newman's poem, we accompany him from his deathbed to his judgment.

After its publication in the Jesuit-run periodical the *Month*, later the same year, it attracted praise from many quarters. Thomas Brown, the Catholic Bishop of Newport, was one who wrote to Newman to express his admiration. Six years earlier he had been the cause of Newman's coming under suspicion in Rome by reporting him to the authorities there for his views on the place of the laity in the Church. Newman, in acknowledging Brown's letter, observed, "It is a great gratification to me to receive your Lordship's approbation on any thing which I have written" (*L.D.* xxii, 39). We may imagine that he was smiling as he chose his words. Then Gladstone, who was soon to become prime minister for the first time, wrote in 1868, when "The Dream" appeared in a volume of Newman's poems. He told him that he had read "Gerontius" several times, and he compared it to Dante's *Divina Commedia* (*L.D.* xxiv, 7, n.1). And soon afterward Newman's old Oriel friend Richard Church made the same comparison in a review. Newman replied that such praise made him blush and passed it off with a comic reference. "Do you remember the story of bashful and humble Tom Churton?" he asked Church, "how at some great Ashmolean gathering he gently breathed into something that looked like a wind instrument—and what followed?" (*L.D.* xxiv, 42) Church did not; he could only guess.

The poem grew in popularity. Newman heard of a farmer "who took to it, when he was ill—it was to him a prayer or meditation" (*L.D.* xxv, 209). And much later he was moved to learn that General Gordon had used it while in Egypt and had it with him in Khartoum. Gordon had then given it to the *Times* correspondent Frank Power, who was later killed. Power's sister lent Newman the copy for a while (*L.D.* xxxi, 51–52). "What struck me so much in his [Gordon's] use of 'The Dream etc.,'" he told another friend, Frederic Rogers, Lord Blachford, "was that in St Paul's words he 'died daily'—he was always on his deathbed, fulfilling the common advice that we should ever pass the day, as if it was to be our last" (*L.D.* xxxi, 67).

Gordon had come to know about the poem during a long conversation with a friend about death. He had been telling him how his spiritual life had changed when he gazed on his father's lifeless body and found himself thinking, "Is this what we all come to?" His friend told him that some of his ideas reminded him of Newman's "Dream of Gerontius." Gordon then asked for a copy and had one sent on to him. He received it in Egypt and must have read it on the way to the Sudan, marking the text in pencil. These were the markings that took Newman's breath away when he saw them (see *L.D.* xxxi, 51–52).

"Is that what we all come to?" Gordon's question is common, whether asked of others or kept silent. After my ordination as a priest, I was surprised how often people asked me about life after death. It was as though my new state was assumed to give me fresh light on the subject. We find it absorbing. Newman's poem has regularly helped people understand it, but it does not tell the whole story or even pretend to. Newman made the point plainly himself. A priest wrote to him almost at once on the poem's publication, full of praise but regretting the slight mention made of the Blessed Virgin. Newman answered him:

> . . . you do me too much honor, if you think I am to see in a dream everything that *has* to be seen in the *subject* dreamed about. . . . It is not my fault if the sleeper did not dream more. Perhaps something woke him. Dreams are generally fragmentary. I have nothing more to tell. (*L.D.* xxi, 498)

We may be aware of other limitations: in particular, the poem is intensely individualistic and neglects almost completely any reference to the final judgment of the entire human race. Yet it is only a dream, fragmentary, partial; we should not ask of it answers it was never intended to supply. In fact, I suspect that it is so popular because it speaks to our real, personal concerns. Theologians may speculate on the great Last Judgment; most of us are more preoccupied with our own. And in "The Dream" we find that three of our most deeply rooted anxieties are addressed: the fear of perpetual extinction, the fear of judgment, and the fear of what that judgment will entail. To make such a claim for Newman's poem may seem extravagant at first, but often we do not notice what we are hearing at a deeper level. We have to heighten our awareness. Let me set the scene.

(iii)

Gerontius, we know, is not supposed to be a candidate for canonization. Although a believer, he is a man of the world who has committed his share of sins and needs to be forgiven. The opening section of the poem, which takes us to the moment of his death, gives us a portrait of the man. First of all, he is a realist. He recognizes that his end is near; no room is left for self-deception: "Jesu,

Maria—," he exclaims, "I am near to death, and Thou art calling me; I know it now" (*V.V.*, 323). And he calls on his friends to pray for him: "So pray for me, my friends, who have not strength to pray" (*V.V.*, 324).

This need for their prayers is sharpened by his own fear. What does he fear? General Gordon's question, "Is this what we all come to?" expresses it exactly. The terror that grips him is the threat of perpetual extinction, of his annihilation. He speaks of his very being giving way, "As though I was no more a substance now," of his decay as unavoidable, so that he must "drop from out the universal frame / Into that shapeless, scopeless, blank abyss, / That utter nothingness, of which I came" (*V.V.*, 324). His words capture the horror many feel when death approaches.

But Gerontius is not a coward. He rallies bravely: "Rouse thee, my fainting soul, and play the man . . . . Prepare to meet thy God. . . . Use well the interval" (*V.V.*, 325). Nor is this courage bravado. While his friends pray for him, his own appeal to God for mercy soars into a stirring act of faith in the Trinity and the Incarnation of the Son:

> Firmly I believe and truly
>   God is Three, and God is One;
> And I next acknowledge duly
>   Manhood taken by the Son.

He proclaims his trust and hope in the redemption won by the cross of Christ, affirms his veneration for the Church and its teachings, accepts with joy the severance of earthly ties, and concludes in adoration, "To the God of earth and heaven, / Father, Son, and Holy Ghost" (*V.V.*, 327–328). Then the sense of horror returns, and with resignation he appeals to Jesus, Mary, and Joseph and commends himself to God: "Into Thy hands, / O Lord, into Thy hands . . ." (*V.V.*, 330). And he dies. But the question remains: is there anything more? Is this what we all come to?

(iv)

Newman at once begins to supply the answer. It is not just that Gerontius has survived death; it is the character of his new condition. If the root of our fear of death is the fear of annihilation, then that dread is, for Gerontius, laid altogether to rest, for, having died, he discovers not nothingness but a degree of self-possession, of self-awareness, that overwhelms him:

> I went to sleep; and now I am refresh'd,
> A strange refreshment: for I feel in me
> An inexpressive lightness, and a sense
> Of freedom, as I were at length myself,
> And ne'er had been before. (*V.V.*, 331–332)

Here is a suggestion of that full knowledge, that full understanding, that comes from being fully understood (see 1 Cor 13:12). And this wholeness shows itself in various ways. His self-knowledge puts everything into perspective:

> . . . now I am
> So whole of heart, so calm, so self-possess'd,
> With such a full content, and with a sense
> So apprehensive and discriminant,
> As no temptation can intoxicate. (*V.V.*, 338)

Even judgment holds no fears for him:

> Now that the hour is come, my fear is fled;
> And at this balance of my destiny,
> Now close upon me, I can look forward
> With a serenest joy. (*V.V.*, 341)

So the fear of perpetual extinction is dispatched by the presentation of the clear alternative: instead of annihilation we come to know ourselves with a completeness and a perfection never attained before. And this self-knowledge is crucial, for it contains the key to the conquest of the other fears as well, the fear of judgment and the punishment that follows. These fears form an alliance. They make themselves more terrible by creating a dilemma: either annihilation or, if not, an unknown judgment and unspeakable punishment. That is a common, popular perception of our destiny. But if, when we die, we find ourselves revealed completely to ourselves, we discover by that very token that our judgment is not arbitrary. We are not going to be judged, as we may have feared, according to some surprise, unseen syllabus. Our own earthly lives will be the subject of judgment, and our self-knowledge can foresee the verdict. Gerontius looks forward to it with "a serenest joy." A hymn for those who have died, which Newman had composed eight years earlier, had anticipated the same idea:

> For daily falls, for pardon'd crime,
> They joy to undergo
> The shadow of Thy cross sublime,
> The remnant of Thy woe. (*V.V.*, 315)

Judgment will not be alien. Our perfect self-knowledge will invite it, welcome it. We will delight in being purified of every imperfection. But does that resolve the third fear, of what that purification might involve? Even with our present, imperfect self-knowledge, we recognize that we have done wrong, that we have sinned. We must face the consequences, and Catholic tradition speaks of our purification as purgatorial fire. Won't that fire be terrible, fearsome? But in the fire we find the answer to our fear.

We may associate fire with pain and punishment, but fire is also a symbol of love. When we love most deeply, we may say we are afire with love. As his guardian angel warns Gerontius by reminding him of the stigmata experienced by St. Francis of Assisi, to come into the presence of this love is to be refined as by fire:

> There was a mortal who is now above
> In the mid glory: he, when near to die,
> Was given communion with the Crucified,—
> Such, that the Master's very wounds were stamp'd
> Upon his flesh; and, from the agony

> Which thrill'd through body and soul in that
> embrace,
> Learn that the flame of the Everlasting Love
> Doth burn ere it transform. . . .(*V.V.*, 352)

And so Gerontius is brought to judgment, to the punishment he must undergo. In what does it consist? In torture? In gratuitous pain? No. He is judged by the sight of his redeemer, and his purification flows from that. As the angel explains:

> It is the face of the Incarnate God
> Shall smite thee with that keen and subtle pain;
> . . .
>
> The sight of Him will kindle in thy heart
> All tender, gracious, reverential thoughts.
> Thou wilt be sick with love, and yearn for Him,
> And feel as though thou couldst but pity Him,
> That one so sweet should e'er have placed
> Himself
> At disadvantage such, as to be used
> So vilely by a being so vile as thee.
> There is a pleading in His pensive eyes
> Will pierce thee to the quick, and trouble thee.
> And thou wilt hate and loathe thyself; for, though
> Now sinless, thou wilt feel that thou hast sinn'd,
> As never thou didst feel; and wilt desire
> To slink away, and hide thee from His sight:
> And yet wilt have a longing aye to dwell
> Within the beauty of His countenance.
> And these two pains, so counter and so keen,—
> The longing for Him, when thou seest Him not;
> The shame of self at thought of seeing Him,—
> Will be thy veriest, sharpest purgatory.
>
> (*V.V.*, 358, 359–360)

The sight of the Christ will inspire the most profound love and cause both longing for union and shame at wrongdoing. The fire that punishes is welcomed because it is a fire of love that purifies and gives life. It conquers Gerontius utterly.

When he goes before his Judge, he is "scorch'd and shrivell'd" by the holiness of the Crucified, "consum'd, yet quicken'd, by the glance of God" (*V.V.*, 366). His judgment is self-judgment. He is stricken with his unworthiness, overwhelmed by love. He begs to be taken away: "That sooner I may rise, and go above, / And see Him in the truth of everlasting day" (*V.V.*, 367). In the union with God, the fire of love, which in purgatory the angel had warned Gerontius was "without its light" (*V.V.*, 351), now gives light, enlightens, brings understanding, the truth of everlasting day.

Among our many fears, these three—annihilation, judgment, and punishment—wield unnerving power. Newman has mastered them with simplicity. When we die, we do not pass away, nor are we diminished; rather, Newman says, we are at last our true selves. God is love. If we die in his friendship, we are overcome by a love that, like a fire, refines us, transforms us, and draws us into its perfect light.

(v)

A copy of "The Dream of Gerontius" with General Gordon's markings, which Newman was so moved to see, was among the wedding presents given in 1899 to Edward Elgar. He was familiar with the poem already. Some years earlier, in 1892, he had already considered composing an oratorio based on the text, and it was perhaps a chance meeting with lawyer Edward Bellasis, another of Newman's lifelong friends, that spurred him on to begin the work. It was ready for the Birmingham Festival in 1900, and although the first performance was generally judged to be a disaster of choral confusion, the piece itself was acclaimed. Since then, of course, it has come to be counted among Elgar's finest works, not least because the music he composed displayed such sympathy with the vision of divine love that Newman's poem reveals.

That vision guided Newman's life.

Chronology

February 21, 1801 – John Henry Newman is born in London.

1820 – Newman completes his degree at Oxford.

April 12, 1822 – Newman is elected Fellow at Oriel College, Oxford.

May 29, 1825 – Newman is ordained to the Anglican priesthood.

June 16, 1833 – Newman composes his poem, "The Pillar of the Cloud," better known as "Lead, Kindly Light."

July 14, 1833 – John Keble preaches the Assize Sermon at Oxford, beginning, for Newman, the Oxford Movement.

1837 – Newman publishes *Lectures on the Prophetical Office of the Church.*

1839 – Newman studies the history of the Monophysite heresy, prompting doubts about his belief in the *via media* of the Anglican Church.

February 27, 1841 – Newman publishes *Tract 90,* containing his reflections on the Thirty-Nine Articles.

September 25, 1843 – Newman preaches his final sermon as an Anglican priest, "The Parting of Friends."

1845 – Newman publishes his *Essay on the Development of Christian Doctrine.*

October 9, 1845 – Newman is formally received into the Catholic Church by Passionist priest Blessed Dominic Barberi.

May 1846 – Newman is ordained into the Catholic priesthood.

1848 – Newman establishes the Birmingham Oratory.

1851 – Newman is named rector of the Catholic University of Ireland. Also publishes *Lectures on the Present Position of Catholics in England.*

1852 – Newman publishes the first edition of *The Idea of a University.*

November 12, 1858 – Newman resigns as rector of the Catholic University of Ireland.

February 1859 –	Richard Sampson resigns as editor of the Catholic periodical *The Rambler*, prompting Newman to take over the position at the request of his bishop.
1859 –	Newman publishes his essay "On Consulting the Faithful in Matters of Doctrine" in *The Rambler*, prompting an end to his brief tenure as editor.
1864 –	Newman publishes his *Apologia Pro Vita Sua*.
1865 –	Edward Pusey publishes his *Eirenicon*.
January 17, 1865 –	Newman begins writing "The Dream of Gerontius."
January 1866 –	Newman composes his *Letter to Pusey* concerning Catholic teaching on the sanctity of Mary in response to Pusey's *Eirenicon*.
June 29, 1868 –	Pope Piux IX summons the First Vatican Council through his papal bull *Pastor Aeternus*.
December 8, 1869 to – September 1, 1870	The First Vatican Council convenes.
1870 –	Newman publishes *An Essay in Aid of a Grammar of Assent*.
1875 –	Newman publishes his *Letter to the Duke of Norfolk* in response to Prime Minister William Gladstone's claims against Catholic voters.
May 15, 1879 –	Pope Leo XIII elevates Newman to the office of cardinal.
August 11, 1890 –	Newman dies at the Birmingham Oratory.
January 22, 1991 –	Newman is venerated by Pope John Paul II.

Notes

Preface
1.   *L'Osservatore Romano*, Weekly Edition in English, February 7, 2007.

1. Have You Read Any Newman?
1.   Placid Murray, ed., *Newman the Oratorian* (Dublin: Gill & Macmillan, 1969).
2.   Meriol Trevor, *Newman: the Pillar of the Cloud* (vol. i); *Newman: Light in Winter* (vol. ii) (London: Macmillan, 1962).
3.   An approach to the Catholic that places high importance on the superiority and infallibility of the pope.
4.   Trevor, *Newman: Light in Winter*, 486. For more on this theme, see Joyce Sugg, "Did Newman Have a Sense of Humour?", *The Clergy Review* lxviii (1983), 100–105.
5.   To correct the caricature, see David Newsome, *The Convert Cardinals: Newman and Manning* (London: John Murray, 1993).
6.   Owen Chadwick, *The Mind of the Oxford Movement* (London: Adam and Charles Black, 1960), 42.
7.   See Chapter 8, "Strange Providence."
8.   Roderick Strange, *The Catholic Faith* (London: Darton, Longman and Todd: 2001); and *Living Catholicism* (Mahwah, NJ: Paulist Press, 2001).

2. Newman's Path
1.   Feast of Blessed Dominic Barberi, National Calendar of England and Wales, *The Divine Office* iii, 435.
2.   H. J. Jackson (ed.), *Samuel Taylor Coleridge* (Oxford: Oxford University Press, 1985), 594–595.
3.   David Newsome, *Two Classes of Men: Platonism and English Romantic Thought* (London: John Murray, 1974), 72.
4.   Hugh M. de Achaval and J. Derek Holmes (eds.), *The Theological Papers of John Henry Newman on Faith and Certainty* (Oxford: Oxford University Press, 1976), 81.
5.   C. S. Dessain, *John Henry Newman*, (London: Adam and Charles Black, 1966; Oxford: Oxford University Press, 1980), 148. See also *An Essay in Aid of a Grammar of Assent*, 495–496 [318–319].

3. A Mind Alive
1.   Nicholas Lash, "Tides and Twilight: Newman Since Vatican II," in *Newman After a Hundred Years*, ed. Ian Ker and Alan G. Hill (Oxford: Oxford University Press, 1990), 451–452.
2.   Ibid.
3.   C. S. Dessain, *John Henry Newman*, xii.
4.   Wilfrid Ward, *The Life of John Henry Cardinal Newman* (London: Longmans, 1912), 460.
5.   David Newsome, *The Convert Cardinals*, 94–102.
6.   Ibid, 99. For Newsome's treatment of the whole affair, see 94–102. See also Roderick Strange, "Newman and Hampden," *Newman-Studien* XIV (Sigmaringendorf, 1990), 29–40.

7.   R. D. Hampden, *Observations on Religious Dissent* (Oxford, 1835), 19, 20.
8.   R. D. Hampden to J. H. Newman, 14 February 1836, in *The Letters and Diaries of John Henry Newman* v, 235; J. H. Newman, *Elucidations of Dr. Hampden's Theological Statements*, (Oxford, 1836), 41.
9.   Stephen Prickett, *Romanticism and Religion: The Tradition of Coleridge and Wordsworth in the Victorian Church* (Cambridge: Cambridge University Press, 1976), 7.
10. Ibid., 219.
11. For a fuller account, see Roderick Strange, "Dogma and Religious Truth," *Ampleforth Journal* lxxxiii (Summer 1978), 4–11.
12. Wilfrid Ward, *William Ward and the Oxford Movement* (London: Macmillan, 1889), 80.
13. Wilfrid Ward, *William George Ward and the Catholic Revival* (London: Longmans, Green, and Co., 1893), 14.
14. Ibid., 65–66.
15. Wilfrid Ward, *William Ward and the Oxford Movement*, 81.
16. Friedrich von Hügel, *The Mystical Element of Religion as Studied in Saint Catherine of Genoa and Her Friends*, (London: J. M. Dent, 1923), i, 50–55. The prompt for much of what follows comes from Michael Paul Gallagher, S.J., "Faith Development of Seminarians," *Seminary Journal* 4/3 (Winter 1998), 22–33.
17. *Catholic Sermons of Cardinal Newman*, edited at the Birmingham Oratory (London: Burns & Oates, 1957), 121.
18. Ibid., 123, 125–131.
19. Pope Benedict XVI, *Give Yourself to Christ: First Homilies of Pope Benedict XVI* (London: Catholic Truth Society, 2005), 18.
20. John L. Allen, Jr., *The Rise of Benedict XVI* (New York: Doubleday, 2005), 165–166, 174–178.
21. Joseph Ratzinger, "Newman Belongs to the Great Teachers of the Church" in *Benedict XVI and Cardinal Newman*, ed. Peter Jennings (Oxford: Oxford University Press, 2005), 33.

4. Infallible Authority

1.   Thomas F. Stransky and John B. Sheerin, *Doing the Truth in Charity: Statements of Pope Paul VI, Popes John Paul I, John Paul II, and the Secretariat for Promoting Christian Unity, 1964-1980* (New York: Paulist Press, 1982), 273.
2.   Hans Küng, *Infallible?* (London: Doubleday, 1971), 23.
3.   H. E. Manning, *The Vatican Council and its Definitions: A Pastoral Letter to the Clergy* (London, 1870), 65–66; reprinted in Manning, *Petri Privilegium* (London, 1871).
4.   For a fuller account of Newman's view, see C. S. Dessain, "Infallibility: What Newman Taught in Manning's Church" in *Infallibility in the Church*, ed. M. D. Goulder (London: Darton, Longman and Todd 1968), 59–80.
5.   Without mentioning him by name, Newman's influence helped guide my account of infallibility in *The Catholic Faith*, 76–80.
6.   Christopher Butler, *The Theology of Vatican II*, (London: Darton, Longman and Todd, 1981), 93–94.

5. Mary, the Mother of Jesus

1. See Chapter 7, "Seeking Church Unity."
2. E. B. Pusey, *An Eirenicon in a Letter to the Author of "The Christian Year"* (Oxford, 1865).
3. These were Cyril of Jerusalem, Ephrem, Epiphanius, Jerome, Augustine, Peter Chrysologus, and Fulgentius (*Diff.* ii, 39–44).
4. J. H. Newman, *Parochial Sermons* ii (first edition, London, 1835), 146. Later Anglican editions and the uniform edition were altered to read, "What, think you, was the sanctified state of that human nature etc.?" See, for example, the fourth edition (London, 1843), 148, and *Parochial Sermons* ii, 132.
5. Here too I readily acknowledge aspects of Newman's thought running through my account of the Immaculate Conception in *The Catholic Faith*, pp. 171-174.
6. Herbert McCabe, *God Matters* (London: Continuum International Publishing, 1987), 213, 214.
7. Roderick Strange, "The Development of Newman's Marian Thought and Devotion," *One in Christ* xvi (1980), 114–126.
8. E. B. Pusey, *Eirenicon*, 118.
9. Donald Nicholson, "Mary: a Living Tradition in Anglicanism," *The Clergy Review* lxii (1977), 318.
10. Eric Kemp, *Mary and Right Belief in Christ* (1975), quoted in Nicholson, "Mary: a Living Tradition in Anglicanism," 322.
11. See also Bishop William Ullathorne's letter to the editor of the *Tablet* in *The Letters and Diaries of John Henry Newman* xxii, 341-344, on Newman's devotion to the Blessed Virgin.
12. A. M. Ramsey, "The Significance of Newman Today" in *The Rediscovery of Newman*, ed. John Coulson and A. M. Allchin (London: Sheed & Ward, 1967), 8.

6. Serving the Laity

1. Peter Hebblethwaite, *John XXIII, Pope of the Council* (London: Continuum International Publishing, 1984), 461.
2. See the edition produced by John Coulson in 1961; it was reprinted in 1986; John Coulson, ed., *John Henry Newman: On Consulting the Faithful in Matters of Doctrine*, (1961; London: HarperCollins, 1986).
3. See Chapter 1, Have You Read Any Newman?
4. A. J. Engel, *From Clergyman to Don: the Rise of the Academic Profession in Nineteenth-Century Oxford* (Oxford: Oxford University Press, 1983), 25.
5. Joyce Sugg, *Ever Yours Affly: John Henry Newman and his Female Circle* (Leominster, United Kingdom: Gracewing, 1996).
6. Roderick Strange, *The Risk of Discipleship* (London: Darton, Longman and Todd, 2004), 161.
7. Placid Murray, ed., *Newman the Oratorian*, 275.
8. J. M. Roberts, "The Idea of a University Revisited" in *Newman After a Hundred Years*, Ker and Hill, eds., 193–222. For a related but more positive view, see Nicholas Lash, "'A Seat of Wisdom, a Light of the World': Considering the University," *Louvain Studies* xv (1990), 188–202.
9. Roderick Strange, *Living Catholicism*, 125–126.
10. Roderick Strange, *The Risk of Discipleship*, 50–53.
11. See in particular, John Coulson, *Newman and the Common Tradition* (Oxford: Oxford University Press, 1970), 113–131.

12. John Coulson, ed., _On Consulting_, 73–75.
13. Quoted in the note on John Gillow in _The Letters and Diaries of John Henry Newman_ xix, 586.
14. See Chapter 2, "Newman's Path."
15. John Coulson, ed., _On Consulting_, 103–104.
16. Ibid., 106.
17. John Coulson, _Newman and the Common Tradition_, 96.
18. John Coulson, ed., _On Consulting_, 47–48.

7. _Seeking Church Unity_

1. H. P. Liddon, _The Life of Edward Bouverie Pusey_, 4 vols., (London, 1893–1897), ii.
2. Ibid., 461.
3. John Coulson and A. M. Allchin, eds., _The Rediscovery of Newman_, xi.
4. C. S. Dessain, "Cardinal Newman and Ecumenism," _The Clergy Review_ l (1965) 119–137, 189–206; see especially 129ff.
5. See Chapter 5, "Mary, the Mother of Jesus."
6. Quoted in David Newsome, _The Convert Cardinals_, 257.
7. Review by David Livingstone, _Sunday Sequence_, BBC Radio Ulster, March 23, 1986.
8. Ibid.
9. See Chapter 5, "Mary, the Mother of Jesus."
10. Quoted in H. P. Liddon, _Life of Edward Bouverie Pusey_, iv, 112.
11. H. E. Manning, _The Workings of the Holy Spirit in the Church of England: a Letter to the Rev. E.B. Pusey, D.D._ (London, 1865), 6–7.
12. E. B. Pusey, _An Eirenicon in a Letter to the Author of "The Christian Year"_ (London, 1865).
13. Ibid., 158–159.
14. Ibid., 169–172.
15. R. W. Church, "An Eirenicon" in _Occasional Papers_ (London, 1897), i, 354.
16. H. P. Liddon, _Life of Pusey_, iv, 121–123.
17. Ibid., 125.
18. E. B. Pusey to Newman, 13 November 1865, in _Newman at Oxford_, R. D. Middleton (London: Oxford University Press, 1950), 250–251.
19. See Chapter 5, "Mary, the Mother of Jesus."
20. H. P. Liddon, _Life of Pusey_, iv, 131.
21. Ibid., 136.
22. R. W. Church, _Occasional Papers_, ii, 406.
23. Ibid., 415.
24. See Chapter 6, "Serving the Laity."

8. _Strange Providence_

1. See Chapter 7, "Seeking Church Unity."
2. Roderick Strange, _Living Catholicism_, 73–78.
3. Lord Byron, _Don Juan_, canto xiv, stanza 101.
4. See Chapter 3, "A Mind Alive," 4–5; see also Stephen Prickett, _Romanticism and Religion_, 114–119.
5. See Chapter 1, "Have You Read Any Newman?"
6. Roderick Strange, _Living Catholicism_, 77–78; 46–49.

9. Preaching the Living Faith

1. Matthew Arnold, "Emerson" in *Philistinism in England and America*, ed. R. H. Super (Ann Arbor, MI: University of Michigan Press, 1974), 165.
2. C. S. Dessain, *John Henry Newman*, xii; see Chapter 3, "A Mind Alive."
3. Owen Chadwick, *The Mind of the Oxford Movement*, 42; see Chapter 1, "Have You Read Any Newman?"
4. See Chapter 1, "Have You Read Any Newman?"; Chapter 2, "Newman's Path."

10. Witness to Holiness

1. See Chapter 1, "Have You Read Any Newman?"
2. The situation, of course, has moved on since the Second Vatican Council ended in 1965. To explore the matter further, compare B. C. Butler, "Newman and the Second Vatican Council" in *The Rediscovery of Newman*, ed. Coulson and Allchin, 233–246; and Nicholas Lash, "Tides and Twilight: Newman Since Vatican II" in *Newman After a Hundred Years*, ed. Ker and Hill, 447–464.
3. See Preface.
4. Roderick Strange, *The Catholic Faith*, 29–31.
5. William Roper, *Life of More* (London: Blackie and Son, 1938), 50.
6. Ibid., 70.
7. Wilfrid Ward, *The Life of Cardinal Newman* ii, 537.

Glossary

Assent

Newman defines assent simply as an "absolute acceptance of a proposition without any condition." In his *Grammar of Assent*, Newman details the process of assent as the questioning of a proposition, the conclusion of this questioning, acceptance of its truth, and then belief. This reasoning process leads to apprehension (acceptance of the truth a proposition declares) and then assent (unconditional belief).

Assent can also be further categorized by the nature of its object. First, there is notional assent. This comprises those propositions concerned with notions, opinions, presumptions, assumptions, and speculations. Notional assent deals with the abstract, which for Newman was weaker and less affecting than the concrete propositions characteristic of the other line of apprehension and assent—real. While notional assent focuses on our own intellectual creations, real assent handles those things (e.g. experience, sensory perception) that have left impressions on us. Despite these differences, the nature of assent as indivisible, unconditional belief remains the same.

Ex Cathedra

Translated literally from Latin to mean "from the chair," *ex cathedra* signifies a teaching coming from the Holy See that is given infallibly. More specifically dealing with faith and morals, a doctrine delivered *ex cathedra* is to be accepted by the Catholic Church as truth, given with divine assistance and rooted, as Newman proclaimed in his *Letter to the Duke of Norfolk*, in the life of the Church.

Illative Sense

Simply stated, the illative sense refers to the human capacity for reasoning. Newman argued that there is an impossibility in ascertaining incontrovertible proof of a proposition in concrete life. In order to overcome this problem, we use converging probabilities. The illative sense discerns the order of these probabilities concerning a certain proposition to arrive at certitude, or recognition of the truth of a proposition.

The illative sense is extremely crucial for Newman's prognosis of assent and belief. The gap created by imperfect proof in the concrete world between converging probabilities and assent must be bridged. The illative sense, as it patterns these probabilities against each other and arrives at certitude on the matter, compensates accordingly, allowing for assent on very critical matters.

Immaculate Conception

Defined as dogma by Pope Pius IX on December 8, 1854, the teaching behind the Immaculate Conception is that Mary, the mother of Jesus, was filled with a divine grace and thus was born without original sin and lived a life completely free from sin.

Infallibility
Typically meaning free from error, papal infallibility is the Catholic doctrine defined during the First Vatican Council in 1870 that states in matters of faith and morals, teachings from the pope given *ex cathedra* are immune from the possibility of error and do not need to be ratified by the Church to be considered truth.

A point of controversy for many Catholics and non-Catholics alike, papal infallibility was a subject Newman sought to clarify for many confused believers and critics. For Newman, one critical aspect of the doctrine is that infallibility is an external gift that rests with the office and not an internal quality within the individual person. In other words, the pope is infallible in matters of faith and morals because the papal office shares in the infallibility of the Church, which is divinely inspired by the Holy Spirit and established through tradition and scripture. Newman used his interpretation of the doctrine in his *Letter to the Duke of Norfolk*, where he responded to ousted prime minister William Gladstone, who accused his election loss to the Catholic vote being overly influenced by an adversarial, infallible pope.

Liberalism
An attitude of openness, tolerance, and individual liberty whose modern origins are typically traced back to the Renaissance in the fourteenth through the seventeenth centuries. The focus on individual rights within liberalism have often contrasted, philosophically, with Catholic belief, particularly when it comes to the importance of obedience and authority within the Church.

Despite these differences, however, many Catholics, including Newman, see the many positives surrounding liberalism, including freedom from tyranny and justice—social and ideological ideals touted by Catholic moral teaching. In the nineteenth century, though, Newman viewed liberalism as a potentially serious danger. An extreme emphasis on tolerance, characteristic within the liberal approach, signaled, for Newman, a weakening of the belief in the objective truths established in the creed and in Church doctrine. Newman's concern over such openness, as well as his critique of more strongly authoritarian Catholics, placed him at odds with both ends of the religious and philosophical spectrum of his time.

Oxford Movement
Beginning in the 1830s, the Oxford Movement aimed at demonstrating the apostolic origins of the Anglican Church of England. For Newman, the movement could be said to have begun with John Keble's Assize Sermon at Oxford in 1833, in which the controversy over state control of the church was addressed.

At its earliest stages, Newman was the driving force behind the movement, believing as he did at the time that the High Anglican Church was part of the greater Church Catholic, joining the Roman and Eastern factions. However,

Newman also saw the integrity and identity of the church under attack by liberalism. In response, the movement sought a *via media*, or middle way, between the errors of the Roman Catholic Church and Protestantism, each of these occupying a differing, faulty extreme. The Oxford Movement featured numerous sermons and tracts, the latter of which became the inspiration behind its other name, the Tractarian Movement.

Revelation
Disclosure of a divine truth through God. A central tenet to Newman's perception of Christianity and religious faith, revelation in the Christian sense comes to the believer through sacred scripture.

Through his search for religion, Newman's focus was on how to best receive revelation. Revealed religion must embody not only the ability to receive and accept revelation (faith), but it must also possess the means to focus and define it (dogma). Newman's controversial quest for such a religion led him to the Catholic Church.

Ultramontanism
An approach to the Catholic faith that places extreme importance on the authority of the pope, ultramontanism became popular with many of Newman's fellow Anglican converts to Catholicism, including W.G. Ward and Henry Cardinal Manning.

At its extreme, ultramontanism asserts belief in the supreme authority of the pope over other lines in the Church hierarchy, including local bishops. For many ultramontanes, the First Vatican Council marked a highpoint in the Church's history, defining the doctrine of papal infallibility as central to Church teaching.

Bibliography

Athanasius, Saint, Patriarch of Alexandria. *Select Treatises of St. Athanasius in Controversy with the Arians.* Trans. John Henry Newman. New York: Green and Co., 1911.

Newman, John Henry. *Apologia pro Vita Sua.* New York: Norton, 1968.

———. *The Arians of the Fourth Century.* Notre Dame, IN: University of Notre Dame Press, 2001.

———. *Autobiographical Writings.* New York: Sheed and Ward, 1957.

———. *Discourses Addressed to Mixed Congregations.* Notre Dame IN: University of Notre Dame, 2002.

———. *Discussions and Arguments on Various Subjects.* Notre Dame, IN, University of Notre Dame Press, 2004.

———. *An Essay on the Development of Christian Doctrine.* Notre Dame, IN: University of Notre Dame Press, 1989.

———. *Certain Difficulties Felt By Anglicans in Catholic Teaching.* New York: Green and Co., 1891-1894.

———. *An Essay in Aid of a Grammar of Assent.* New York: Oxford University Press, 1985.

———. *Essays Critical and Historical.* London: Longmans, 1890.

———.*Fifteen Sermons Preached Before the University of Oxford.* Oxford: Oxford University Press, 2006.

———. *Historical Sketches.* London: Longman, Greens and Co., 1897-1899.

———. *The Idea of a University: defined and illustrated in nine discourses delivered to the Catholics of Dublin in occasional lectures and essays addressed to the members of the Catholic University.* Notre Dame, IN: University of Notre Dame Press, 1982.

———. *Lectures on the Doctrine of Justification.* New York: Scribner, Welford, and Armstrong, 1874.

———. *Lectures on the Present Position of Catholics in England.* Notre Dame, IN: University of Notre Dame Press, 2000.

———. *Meditations and Devotions of the Late Cardinal Newman.* London: Longmans, Green, and co., 1893.

———. *Parochial and Plain Sermons.* San Francisco: Ignatius Press, 1987.

———. *Sermons Bearing on Subjects of the Day.* London: Longmans, Green, and Co., 1909.

———. *Sermons Preached on Various Occasions.* London: Longmans, Green, 1921.

———. *Tracts Theological and Ecclesiastical.* London: Pickering, 1881.

———. *Verses on various occasions.* London: Longmans, Green, 1890.

———. *The Via Media of the Anglican Church.* New York: Oxford University Press, 1990.

Index

Monsignor Roderick Strange has been reading and studying Newman for over forty years and has felt Newman's heavy influence on him personally, spiritually, and intellectually. Strange is the current rector of Beda College in Rome. He has served in the position for nearly ten years, guiding men from all over the world into the priesthood. He has been a university chaplain at Oxford University, a parish priest in Cheshire, England, and chairman of the National Conference of Priests. He is the author of *The Catholic Faith, Living Catholicism* and *The Risk of Discipleship*.

Other Books in the *101* Series

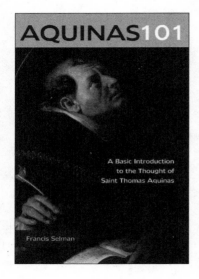

Aquinas 101
A Basic Introduction to the Thought
of Saint Thomas Aquinas
Francis Selman

This brief, engaging, and readable summary of the influential thought of St. Thomas Aquinas takes complex, confusing topics and thoughtfully, yet clearly, summarizes the legacy of one of the Catholic Church's greatest minds. *No longer is St. Thomas the reserve of upper-level, esoteric courses. Now he can be studied by the "beginners" he cared so much for.* —**Mark Johnson, PhD,** Professor of Theology, Marquette University

ISBN: 9780870612435 / 224 pages / $15.95

Available from your bookstore or from
ave maria press / Notre Dame, IN 46556
www.avemariapress.com / Ph: 800-282-1865
A Ministry of the Indiana Province of Holy Cross

Keycode: FD9Ø6Ø8ØØØØ